The Ethics of Belief

Essays by
William Kingdon Clifford
William James
A.J. Burger

Edited by A.J. Burger

Revised Edition

The Ethics of Belief
Edited by A.J. Burger

Essays by
William Kingdon Clifford
William James
A.J. Burger

Revised Edition

Printed on acid-free paper.

ISBN-13/EAN-13: 978-1-43-825176-9

ISBN 1-438251-76-9

Publisher's Cataloging-in-Publication Data
  A J Burger
  The Ethics of Belief: Essays by William K Clifford,
William James, and A J Burger / Edited by A J Burger
    p.   cm.
  ISBN 1-438251-76-9
    1. William Kingdon Clifford, 1845-1879. 2. William
James, 1842-1910. 3. A.J. Burger. 4. Ethics. 5. Religion.
6. Truth.

I. William Kingdon Clifford. II. William James. III. A J
Burger. IV. Title.
B945.J24   Dewey: 141

CONTENTS

CONTENTS

Preface

People have long been interested in the circumstances under which it is appropriate to believe. Often, the source of this interest is the desire to believe something for which one has insufficient evidence. Extensive excerpts of the following essays by William Kingdon Clifford and William James are often reprinted in anthologies. This is sufficient proof of the enduring interest in this subject, and of the importance of these particular essays. But since they are *excerpts*, and since Clifford's *Lectures and Essays* is no longer in print, there is a need for the present book. Indeed, usually the excerpts from Clifford's essay come exclusively from part *one* of his *three-part* essay. And James' essay is usually reprinted without parts II, III, V, VI, and VII, with the other parts not reprinted in their entirety. Following are "The Ethics of Belief" and "The Will to Believe" in their entirety, along with added explanatory notes. Following these essays is "An Examination of 'The Will to Believe.'" It is not the first examination of that work;[1] however, it is, I believe, one that adds a unique contribution to the discussion. The reader is advised to read the essays in the order presented here (which is the order in which they were written), as James' essay is a response to Clifford's essay,

[1] See, for example, *A History of Western Philosophy* by Bertrand Russell (Simon & Schuster, 1945), ch. XXIX, particularly p 814-816; and "The Dark Side of Religion" in *The Faith of a Liberal* by Morris R. Cohen (Henry Holt, 1946), a relevant section of which is also reprinted as "Religion and the Will to Believe" in *Introductory Readings in Philosophy*, Marcus G. Singer and Robert R. Ammerman, eds. (Charles Scribner's Sons, 1962), p 231-234, and also as "A Critique of the Will to Believe" in *Decisions in Philosophy of Religion*, William B. Williamson, ed. (Prometheus Books, 1985), p 125-128.

as well as to ideas of a like nature; and my own essay is a response to James' essay.

It is to be hoped that the present volume will be useful to anyone interested in the question of whether it is appropriate to have *faith*—that is, believe in the absence of evidence. Indeed, even if my own essay is not as useful as I believe it to be, the availability of Clifford's and James' essays, reprinted in their entirety, in one convenient book, should prove worthwhile.

A.J. Burger
September 2001

About the Text

The text of William Kingdon Clifford's "The Ethics of Belief" is based upon the first edition of *Lectures and Essays*, Macmillan and Co., 1879, edited by Leslie Stephen and Frederick Pollock. The text of William James' "The Will to Believe" is based upon the first edition of *The Will to Believe and other essays in popular philosophy*, Longmans, Green and Co., 1897. In the essays by Clifford and James, the added footnotes are indicated by "*—AJB*". This is the first printing of "An Examination of 'The Will to Believe,'" which was originally written in 1994, and has been subsequently revised.

Revised Edition
2008

This revised edition is the same as the original edition, with the exception that an "Afterword" has been added.

The Ethics of Belief

1879

William Kingdon Clifford

THE ETHICS OF BELIEF.[1]

I.—The Duty of Inquiry.

A SHIPOWNER was about to send to sea an emigrant-ship. He knew that she was old, and not over-well built at the first; that she had seen many seas and climes, and often had needed repairs. Doubts had been suggested to him that possibly she was not seaworthy. These doubts preyed upon his mind, and made him unhappy; he thought that perhaps he ought to have her thoroughly overhauled and refitted, even though this should put him to great expense. Before the ship sailed, however, he succeeded in overcoming these melancholy reflections. He said to himself that she had gone safely through so many voyages and weathered so many storms that it was idle to suppose she would not come safely home from this trip also. He would put his trust in Providence, which could hardly fail to protect all these unhappy families that were leaving their fatherland to seek for better times elsewhere. He would dismiss from his mind all ungenerous suspicions about the honesty of

---

[1] *Contemporary Review*, January, 1877.

builders and contractors.   In such ways he acquired a sincere and comfortable conviction that his vessel was thoroughly safe and seaworthy; he watched her departure with a light heart, and benevolent wishes for the success of the exiles in their strange new home that was to be; and he got his insurance-money when she went down in mid-ocean and told no tales.

What shall we say of him?   Surely this, that he was verily guilty of the death of those men.   It is admitted that he did sincerely believe in the soundness of his ship; but the sincerity of his conviction can in no wise help him, because *he had no right to believe on such evidence as was before him.*   He had acquired his belief not by honestly earning it in patient investigation, but by stifling his doubts.   And although in the end he may have felt so sure about it that he could not think otherwise, yet inasmuch as he had knowingly and willingly worked himself into that frame of mind, he must be held responsible for it.

Let us alter the case a little, and suppose that the ship was not unsound after all; that she made her voyage safely, and many others after it.   Will that diminish the guilt of her owner?   Not one jot.   When an action is once done, it is right or wrong for ever; no accidental failure of its good or evil fruits can possibly alter that.   The man would not have been innocent, he would only have been not found out.   The question of right or wrong has to do with the origin of his belief, not the matter of it; not what it was, but how he got it; not whether it turned out to be true or false, but whether he had a right to believe on such evidence as was before him.

There was once an island in which some of the inhabitants professed a religion teaching neither the doctrine of original sin nor that of eternal punishment.   A suspicion got abroad that the professors of this religion had made use of unfair means to get their doctrines taught to children. They were accused of wresting the laws of their country in such a way as to remove children from the care of their natural and legal guardians; and even of stealing them away and keeping them concealed from their friends and relations. A certain number of men formed themselves into a society for the purpose of agitating the public about this matter. They published grave accusations against individual citizens of the highest position and character, and did all in their power to injure these citizens in the exercise of their professions. So great was the noise they made, that a Commission was appointed to investigate the facts; but after the Commission had carefully inquired into all the evidence that could be got, it appeared that the accused were innocent. Not only had they been accused on insufficient evidence, but the evidence of their innocence was such as the agitators might easily have obtained, if they had attempted a fair inquiry. After these disclosures the inhabitants of that country looked upon the members of the agitating society, not only as persons whose judgment was to be distrusted, but also as no longer to be counted honourable men. For although they had sincerely and conscientiously believed in the charges they had made, yet *they had no right to believe on such evidence as was before them.* Their sincere convictions, instead of being honestly earned by patient inquiring, were stolen by listening to the voice of prejudice and passion.

Let us vary this case also, and suppose, other things remaining as before, that a still more accurate investigation proved the accused to have been really guilty. Would this make any difference in the guilt of the accusers? Clearly not; the question is not whether their belief was true or false, but whether they entertained it on wrong grounds. They would no doubt say, 'Now you see that we were right after all; next time perhaps you will believe us.' And they might be believed, but they would not thereby become honourable men. They would not be innocent, they would only be not found out. Every one of them, if he chose to examine himself *in foro conscientiæ*, would know that he had acquired and nourished a belief, when he had no right to believe on such evidence as was before him; and therein he would know that he had done a wrong thing.

It may be said, however, that in both of these supposed cases it is not the belief which is judged to be wrong, but the action following upon it. The shipowner might say, 'I am perfectly certain that my ship is sound, but still I feel it my duty to have her examined, before trusting the lives of so many people to her.' And it might be said to the agitator, 'However convinced you were of the justice of your cause and the truth of your convictions, you ought not to have made a public attack upon any man's character until you had examined the evidence on both sides with the utmost patience and care.'

In the first place, let us admit that, so far as it goes, this view of the case is right and necessary; right, because even when a man's belief is so fixed that he cannot think otherwise, he still has a choice in regard to the action suggested by it, and so cannot escape the duty of investigating on the ground of the strength of his convictions; and necessary, because those who are not yet capable of controlling their feelings and thoughts must have a plain rule dealing with overt acts.

But this being premised as necessary, it becomes clear that it is not sufficient, and that our previous judgment is required to supplement it. For it is not possible so to sever the belief from the action it suggests as to condemn the one without condemning the other. No man holding a strong belief on one side of a question, or even wishing to hold a belief on one side, can investigate it with such fairness and completeness as if he were really in doubt and unbiassed; so that the existence of a belief not founded on fair inquiry unfits a man for the performance of this necessary duty.

Nor is that truly a belief at all which has not some influence upon the actions of him who holds it. He who truly believes that which prompts him to an action has looked upon the action to lust after it, he has committed it already in his heart. If a belief is not realized immediately in open deeds, it is stored up for the guidance of the future. It goes to make a part of that aggregate of beliefs which is the link between sensation and action at every moment of all our lives, and which is so organized and compacted together that no part of it can be isolated from the rest, but every new addition modifies the structure of the whole. No real belief, however trifling and fragmentary it may seem, is ever truly insignificant; it prepares us to receive more of its like, confirms those which resembled it before, and weakens others; and so gradually it lays a stealthy train in our inmost thoughts, which may some day explode into overt action, and leave its stamp upon our character for ever.

And no one man's belief is in any case a private matter which concerns himself alone. Our lives are guided by that general conception of the course of things which has been created by society for social purposes. Our words, our phrases, our forms and processes and modes of thought, are common property, fashioned and perfected from age to age; an heirloom which every succeeding generation inherits as a precious deposit and a sacred trust to be handed on to the next one, not unchanged but enlarged and purified, with some clear marks of its proper handiwork. Into this, for good or ill, is woven every belief of every man who has speech of his fellows. An awful privilege, and an awful responsibility, that we should help to create the world in which posterity will live.

In the two supposed cases which have been considered, it has been judged wrong to believe on insufficient evidence, or to nourish belief by suppressing doubts and avoiding investigation. The reason of this judgment is not far to seek: it is that in both these cases the belief held by one man was of great importance to other men. But forasmuch as no belief held by one man, however seemingly trivial the belief, and however obscure the believer, is ever actually insignificant or without its effect on the fate of mankind, we have no choice but to extend our judgment to all cases of belief whatever. Belief, that sacred faculty which prompts the decisions of our will, and knits into harmonious working all the compacted energies of our being, is ours not for ourselves, but for humanity. It is rightly used on truths which have been established by long experience and waiting toil, and which have stood in the fierce light of free and fearless questioning. Then it helps to bind men together, and to strengthen and direct their common action. It is desecrated when given to unproved and unquestioned statements, for the solace and private pleasure of the believer; to add a tinsel splendour to the plain straight road of our life and display a bright mirage beyond it; or even to drown the common sorrows of our kind by a self-deception which allows them not only to cast down, but also to degrade us. Whoso would deserve well of his fellows in this matter will guard the purity of his belief with a very fanaticism of jealous care, lest at any time it should rest on an unworthy object, and catch a stain which can never be wiped away.

It is not only the leader of men, statesmen, philosopher, or poet, that owes this bounden duty to mankind. Every rustic who delivers in the village alehouse his slow, infrequent sentences, may help to kill or keep alive the fatal superstitions which clog his race. Every hard-worked wife of an artisan may transmit to her children beliefs which shall knit society together, or rend it in pieces. No simplicity of mind, no obscurity of station, can escape the universal duty of questioning all that we believe.

It is true that this duty is a hard one, and the doubt which comes out of it is often a very bitter thing. It leaves us bare and powerless where we thought that we were safe and strong. To know all about anything is to know how to deal with it under all circumstances. We feel much happier and more secure when we think we know precisely what to do, no matter what happens, than when we have lost our way and do not know where to turn. And if we have supposed ourselves to know all about anything, and to be capable of doing what is fit in regard to it, we naturally do not like to find that we are really ignorant and powerless, that we have to begin again at the beginning, and try to learn what the thing is and how it is to be dealt with—if indeed anything can be learnt about it. It is the sense of power attached to a sense of knowledge that makes men desirous of believing, and afraid of doubting.

This sense of power is the highest and best of pleasures when the belief on which it is founded is a true belief, and has been fairly earned by investigation. For then we may justly feel that it is common property, and holds good for others as well as for ourselves. Then we may be glad, not that *I* have learned secrets by which I am safer and stronger, but that *we men* have got mastery over more of the world; and we shall be strong, not for ourselves, but in the name of Man and in his strength. But if the belief has been accepted on insufficient evidence, the pleasure is a stolen one. Not only does it deceive ourselves by giving us a sense of power which we do not really possess, but it is sinful, because it is stolen in defiance of our duty to mankind. That duty is to guard ourselves from such beliefs as from a pestilence, which may shortly master our own body and then spread to the rest of the town. What would be thought of one who, for the sake of a sweet fruit, should deliberately run the risk of bringing a plague upon his family and his neighbours?

And, as in other such cases, it is not the risk only which has to be considered; for a bad action is always bad at the time when it is done, no matter what happens afterwards. Every time we let ourselves believe for unworthy reasons, we weaken our powers of self-control, of doubting, of judicially and fairly weighing evidence. We all suffer severely enough from the maintenance and support of false beliefs and the fatally wrong actions which they lead to, and the evil born when one such belief is entertained is great and wide. But a greater and wider evil arises when the credulous character is maintained and supported, when a habit of believing for unworthy reasons is fostered and made permanent. If I steal money from any person, there may be no harm done by the mere transfer of possession; he may not feel the loss, or it may prevent him from using the money badly. But I cannot help doing this great wrong towards Man, that I make myself dishonest. What hurts society is not that it should lose its property, but that it should become a den of thieves; for then it must cease to be society. This is why we ought not to do evil that good may come; for at any rate this great evil has come, that we have done evil and are made wicked thereby. In like manner, if I let myself believe anything on insufficient evidence, there may be no great harm done by the mere belief; it may be true after all, or I may never have occasion to exhibit it in outward acts. But I cannot help doing this great wrong towards Man, that I make myself credulous. The danger to society is not merely that it should believe wrong things, though that is great enough; but that it should become credulous, and lose the habit of testing things and inquiring into them; for then it must sink back into savagery.

The harm which is done by credulity in a man is not confined to the fostering of a credulous character in others, and consequent support of false beliefs. Habitual want of care about what I believe leads to habitual want of care in others about the truth of what is told to me. Men speak the truth to one another when each reveres the truth in his own mind and in the other's mind; but how shall my friend revere the truth in my mind when I myself am careless about it, when I believe things because I want to believe them, and because they are comforting and pleasant? Will he not learn to cry, 'Peace,' to me, when there is no peace? By such a course I shall surround myself with a thick atmosphere of falsehood and fraud, and in that I must live. It may matter little to me, in my cloud-castle of sweet illusions and darling lies; but it matters much to Man that I have made my neighbours ready to deceive. The credulous man is father to the liar and the cheat; he lives in the bosom of this his family, and it is no marvel if he should become even as they are. So closely are our duties knit together, that whoso shall keep the whole law, and yet offend in one point, he is guilty of all.

To sum up: it is wrong always, everywhere, and for anyone, to believe anything upon insufficient evidence.

If a man, holding a belief which he was taught in childhood or persuaded of afterwards, keeps down and pushes away any doubts which arise about it in his mind, purposely avoids the reading of books and the company of men that call in question or discuss it, and regards as impious those questions which cannot easily be asked without disturbing it—the life of that man is one long sin against mankind.

If this judgment seems harsh when applied to those simple souls who have never known better, who have been brought up from the cradle with a horror of doubt, and taught that their eternal welfare depends on *what* they believe, then it leads to the very serious question, *Who hath made Israel to sin?*

It may be permitted me to fortify this judgment with the sentence of Milton[1]—

'A man may be a heretic in the truth; and if he believe things only because his pastor says so, or the assembly so determine, without knowing other reason, though his belief be true, yet the very truth he holds becomes his heresy.'

And with this famous aphorism of Coleridge[2]—

'He who begins by loving Christianity better than Truth, will proceed by loving his own sect or Church better than Christianity, and end in loving himself better than all.'

Inquiry into the evidence of a doctrine is not to be made once for all, and then taken as finally settled. It is never lawful to stifle a doubt; for either it can be honestly

[1] *Areopagitica.*
[2] *Aids to Reflection.*

answered by means of the inquiry already made, or else it proves that the inquiry was not complete.

'But,' says one, 'I am a busy man; I have no time for the long course of study which would be necessary to make me in any degree a competent judge of certain questions, or even able to understand the nature of the arguments.' Then he should have no time to believe.

II.—*The Weight of Authority.*

Are we then to become universal sceptics, doubting everything, afraid always to put one foot before the other until we have personally tested the firmness of the road? Are we to deprive ourselves of the help and guidance of that vast body of knowledge which is daily growing upon the world, because neither we nor any other one person can possibly test a hundredth part of it by immediate experiment or observation, and because it would not be completely proved if we did? Shall we steal and tell lies because we have had no personal experience wide enough to justify the belief that it is wrong to do so?

There is no practical danger that such consequences will ever follow from scrupulous care and self-control in the matter of belief. Those men who have most nearly done their duty in this respect have found that certain great principles, and these most fitted for the guidance of life, have stood out more and more clearly in proportion to the care and honesty with which they were tested, and have acquired in this way a practical certainty. The beliefs about right and wrong which guide our actions in dealing with men in society, and the beliefs about physical nature which guide our actions in dealing with animate and inanimate bodies, these never suffer from investigation; they can take care of themselves, without being propped up by 'acts of faith,' the clamour of paid advocates, or the suppression of contrary evidence. Moreover there are many cases in which it is our duty to act upon probabilities, although the evidence is not such as to justify present belief; because it is precisely by such action, and by observation of its fruits, that evidence is got which may justify future belief. So that we have no reason to fear lest a habit of conscientious inquiry should paralyse the actions of our daily life.

But because it is not enough to say, 'It is wrong to believe on unworthy evidence,' without saying also what evidence is worthy, we shall now go on to inquire under what circumstances it is lawful to believe on the testimony of others; and then, further, we shall inquire more generally when and why we may believe that which goes beyond our own experience, or even beyond the experience of mankind.

In what cases, then, let us ask in the first place, is the testimony of a man unworthy of belief? He may say that which is untrue either knowingly or unknowingly. In the first case he is lying, and his moral character is to blame; in the second case he is ignorant or mistaken, and it is only his knowledge or his judgment which is in fault. In order that we may have the right to accept his testimony as ground for believing what he says, we must have reasonable grounds for trusting his *veracity*, that he is really trying to speak the truth so far as he knows it; his *knowledge*, that he has had opportunities of knowing the truth about this matter; and his *judgment*, that he has made proper use of those opportunities in coming to the conclusion which he affirms.

However plain and obvious these reasons may be, so that no man of ordinary intelligence, reflecting upon the matter, could fail to arrive at them, it is nevertheless true that a great many persons do habitually disregard them in weighing testimony. Of the two questions, equally important to the trustworthiness of a witness, 'Is he dishonest?' and 'May he be mistaken?' the majority of mankind are perfectly satisfied if *one* can, with some show of probability, be answered in the negative. The excellent moral character of a man is alleged as ground for accepting his statements about things which he cannot possibly have known. A Mohammedan, for example, will tell us that the character of his Prophet was so noble and majestic that it commands the reverence even of those who do not believe in his mission. So admirable was his moral teaching, so wisely put together the great social machine which he created, that his precepts have not only been accepted by a great portion of mankind, but have actually been obeyed. His institutions have on the one hand rescued the negro from savagery, and on the other hand have taught civilization to the advancing West; and although the races which held the highest forms of his faith, and most fully embodied his mind and thought, have all been conquered and swept away by barbaric tribes, yet the history of their marvellous attainments remains as an imperishable glory to Islam. Are we to doubt the word of a man so great and so good? Can we suppose that this magnificent genius, this splendid moral hero, has lied to us about the most solemn and sacred matters? The testimony of Mohammed is clear, that there is but one God, and that he, Mohammed, is his prophet; that if we believe in him we shall enjoy everlasting felicity, but that if we do not we shall be damned. This testimony rests on the most awful of foundations, the revelation of heaven itself; for was he not visited by the angel Gabriel, as he fasted and prayed in his desert cave, and allowed to enter into the blessed fields of Paradise? Surely God is God and Mohammed is the Prophet of God.

What should we answer to this Mussulman? First, no doubt, we should be tempted to take exception against his view of the character of the Prophet and the uniformly beneficial influence of Islam: before we could go with him altogether in these matters it might seem that we should have to forget many terrible things of which we have heard or read. But if we chose to grant him all these assumptions, for the sake of argument, and because it is difficult both for the faithful and for infidels to discuss them fairly and without passion, still we should have something to say which takes away the ground of his belief, and therefore shows that it is wrong to entertain it. Namely this: the character of Mohammed is excellent evidence that he was honest and spoke the truth so far as he knew it; but it is no evidence at all that he knew what the truth was. What means could he have of knowing that the form which appeared to him to be the angel Gabriel was not a hallucination, and that his apparent visit to Paradise was not a dream? Grant that he himself was fully persuaded and honestly believed that he had the guidance of heaven, and was the vehicle of a supernatural revelation, how could he know that this strong conviction was not a mistake? Let us put ourselves in his place; we shall find that the more completely we endeavour to realise what passed through his mind, the more clearly we shall perceive that the Prophet could have had no adequate ground for the belief in his own inspiration. It is most probable that he himself never doubted of the matter, or thought of asking the question; but we are in the position of those to whom the question has been asked, and who are bound to answer it. It is known to medical observers that solitude and want of food are powerful means of producing delusion and of fostering a tendency to mental disease. Let us suppose, then, that I, like Mohammed, go into desert places to fast and pray; what things can happen to me which will give me the right to believe that I am divinely inspired? Suppose that I get information, apparently from a celestial visitor, which upon being tested is found to be correct. I cannot be sure, in the first place, that the celestial visitor is not a figment of my own mind, and that the information did not come to me, unknown at the time to my consciousness, through some subtle channel of sense. But if my visitor were a real visitor, and for a long time gave me information which was found to be trustworthy, this would indeed be good ground for trusting him in the future as to such matters as fall within human powers of verification; but it would not be ground for trusting his testimony as to any other matters. For although his tested character would justify me in believing that he spoke the truth so far as he knew, yet the same question would present itself—what ground is there for supposing that he knows?

Even if my supposed visitor had given me such information, subsequently verified by me, as proved him to have means of knowledge about verifiable matters far exceeding my own; this would not justify me in believing what he said about matters that are not at present capable of verification by man. It would be ground for interesting conjecture, and for the hope that, as the fruit of our patient inquiry, we might by-and-by attain to such a means of verification as should rightly turn conjecture into belief. For belief belongs to man, and to the guidance of human affairs: no belief is real unless it guide our actions, and those very actions supply a test of its truth.

But, it may be replied, the acceptance of Islam as a system is just that action which is prompted by belief in the mission of the Prophet, and which will serve for a test of its truth.   Is it possible to believe that a system which has succeeded so well is really founded upon a delusion? Not only have individual saints found joy and peace in believing, and verified those spiritual experiences which are promised to the faithful, but nations also have been raised from savagery or barbarism to a higher social state. Surely we are at liberty to say that the belief has been acted upon, and that it has been verified.

It requires, however, but little consideration to show that what has really been verified is not at all the supernal character of the Prophet's mission, or the trustworthiness of his authority in matters which we ourselves cannot test, but only his practical wisdom in certain very mundane things. The fact that believers have found joy and peace in believing gives us the right to say that the doctrine is a comfortable doctrine, and pleasant to the soul; but it does not give us the right to say that it is true. And the question which our conscience is always asking about that which we are tempted to believe is not, 'Is it comfortable and pleasant?' but, 'Is it true?'   That the Prophet preached certain doctrines, and predicted that spiritual comfort would be found in them, proves only his sympathy with human nature and his knowledge of it; but it does not prove his superhuman knowledge of theology.

And if we admit for the sake of argument (for it seems that we cannot do more) that the progress made by Moslem nations in certain cases was really due to the system formed and sent forth into the world by Mohammed, we are not at liberty to conclude from this that he was inspired to declare the truth about things which we cannot verify. We are only at liberty to infer the excellence of his moral precepts, or of the means which he devised for so working upon men as to[1] get them obeyed, or of the social and political machinery which he set up. And it would require a great amount of careful examination into the history of those nations to determine which of these things had the greater share in the result. So that here again it is the Prophet's knowledge of human nature, and his sympathy with it, that are verified; not his divine inspiration, or his knowledge of theology.

If there were only one Prophet, indeed, it might well seem a difficult and even an ungracious task to decide upon what points we would trust him, and on what we would doubt his authority; seeing what help and furtherance all men have gained in all ages from those who saw more clearly, who felt more strongly, and who sought the truth with more single heart than their weaker brethren. But there is not only one Prophet; and while the consent of many upon that which, as men, they had real means of knowing and did know, has endured to the end, and been honourably built into the great fabric of human knowledge, the diverse witness of some about that which they did not and could not know remains as a warning to us that to exaggerate the prophetic authority is to misuse it, and to dishonor those who have sought only to help and further us after their power. It is hardly in human nature that a man should quite accurately gauge the limits of his own insight; but it is the duty of those who profit by his work to consider carefully where he may have been carried beyond it. If we must needs embalm his possible errors along with his solid achievements, and use his authority as an excuse for

---

[1] The first edition has "so" instead of "to", which is an obvious misprint. —*AJB*

believing what he cannot have known, we make of his goodness an occasion to sin.

To consider only one other such witness: the followers of the Buddha have at least as much right to appeal to individual and social experience in support of the authority of the Eastern saviour. The special mark of his religion, it is said, that in which it has never been surpassed, is the comfort and consolation which it gives to the sick and sorrowful, the tender sympathy with which it soothes and assuages all the natural griefs of men. And surely no triumph of social morality can be greater or nobler than that which has kept nearly half the human race from persecuting in the name of religion. If we are to trust the accounts of his early followers, he believed himself to have come upon earth with a divine and cosmic mission to set rolling the wheel of the law. Being a prince, he divested himself of his kingdom, and of his free will became acquainted with misery, that he might learn how to meet and subdue it. Could such a man speak falsely about solemn things? And as for his knowledge, was he not a man miraculous with powers more than man's? He was born of woman without the help of man; he rose into the air and was transfigured before his kinsmen; at last he went up bodily into heaven from the top of Adam's Peak. Is not his word to be believed in when he testifies of heavenly things?

If there were only he, and no other, with such claims! But there is Mohammed with his testimony; we cannot choose but listen to them both. The Prophet tells us that there is one God, and that we shall live for ever in joy or misery, according as we believe in the Prophet or not. The Buddha says that there is no God, and that we shall be annihilated by-and-by if we are good enough. Both cannot be infallibly inspired; one or the other must have been the victim of a delusion, and thought he knew that which he really did not know. Who shall dare to say which? and how can we justify ourselves in believing that the other was not also deluded?

We are led, then, to these judgments following. The goodness and greatness of a man do not justify us in accepting a belief upon the warrant of his authority, unless there are reasonable grounds for supposing that he knew the truth of what he was saying. And there can be no grounds for supposing that a man knows that which we, without ceasing to be men, could not be supposed to verify.

If a chemist tells me, who am no chemist, that a certain substance can be made by putting together other substances in certain proportions and subjecting them to a known process, I am quite justified in believing this upon his authority, unless I know anything against his character or his judgment. For his professional training is one which tends to encourage veracity and the honest pursuit of truth, and to produce a dislike of hasty conclusions and slovenly investigation. And I have reasonable ground for supposing that he knows the truth of what he is saying, for although I am no chemist, I can be made to understand so much of the methods and processes of the science as makes it conceivable to me that, without ceasing to be man, I might verify the statement. I may never actually verify it, or even see any experiment which goes towards verifying it; but still I have quite reason enough to justify me in believing that the verification is within the reach of human appliances and powers, and in particular that it has been actually performed by my informant. His result, the belief to which he has been led by his inquiries, is valid not only for himself but for others; it is watched and tested by those who are working in the same ground, and who know that no greater service can be rendered to science than the purification of accepted results from the errors which may have crept into them. It is in this way that the result becomes common property, a right object of belief, which is a social affair and matter of public business. Thus it is to be observed that his authority is valid because there are those who question it and verify it; that it is precisely this process of examining and purifying that keeps alive among investigators the love of that which shall stand all possible tests, the sense of public responsibility as of those whose work, if well done, shall remain as the enduring heritage of mankind.

But if my chemist tells me that an atom of oxygen has existed unaltered in weight and rate of vibration throughout all time, I have no right to believe this on his authority, for it is a thing which he cannot know without ceasing to be man. He may quite honestly believe that this statement is a fair inference from his experiments, but in that case his judgment is at fault. A very simple consideration of the character of experiments would show him that they never can lead to results of such a kind; that being themselves only approximate and limited, they cannot give us knowledge which is exact and universal. No eminence of character and genius can give a man authority enough to justify us in believing him when he makes statements implying exact or universal knowledge.

Again, an Arctic explorer may tell us that in a given latitude and longitude he has experienced such and such a degree of cold, that the sea was of such a depth, and the ice of such a character. We should be quite right to believe him, in the absence of any stain upon his veracity. It is conceivable that we might, without ceasing to be men, go there and verify his statement; it can be tested by the witness of his companions, and there is adequate ground for supposing that he knows the truth of what he is saying. But if an old whaler tells us that the ice is three hundred feet thick all the way up to the Pole, we shall not be justified in believing him. For although the statement may be capable of verification by man, it is certainly not capable of verification by *him*, with any means and appliances which he has possessed; and he must have persuaded himself of the truth of it by some means which does not attach any credit to his testimony. Even if, therefore, the matter affirmed is within the reach of human knowledge, we have no right to accept it upon authority unless it is within the reach of our informant's knowledge.

What shall we say of that authority, more venerable and august than any individual witness, the time-honoured tradition of the human race? An atmosphere of beliefs and conceptions has been formed by the labours and struggles of our forefathers, which enables us to breathe amid the various and complex circumstances of our life. It is around and about us and within us; we cannot think except in the forms and processes of thought which it supplies. Is it possible to doubt and to test it? and if possible, is it right?

We shall find reason to answer that it is not only possible and right, but our bounden duty; that the main purpose of the tradition itself is to supply us with the means of asking questions, of testing and inquiring into things; that if we misuse it, and take it as a collection of cut-and-dried statements, to be accepted without further inquiry, we are not only injuring ourselves here, but by refusing to do our part towards the building up of the fabric which shall be inherited by our children, we are tending to cut off ourselves and our race from the human line.

Let us first take care to distinguish a kind of tradition which especially requires to be examined and called in question, because it especially shrinks from inquiry. Suppose that a medicine-man in Central Africa tells his tribe that a certain powerful medicine in his tent will be propitiated if they kill their cattle; and that the tribe believe him. Whether the medicine was propitiated or not, there are no means of verifying, but the cattle are gone. Still the belief may be kept up in the tribe that propitiation has been effected in this way; and in a later generation it will be all the easier for another medicine-man to persuade them to a similar act.   Here the only reason for belief is that everybody has believed the thing for so long that it must be true.   And yet the belief was founded on fraud, and has been propagated by credulity.   That man will undoubtedly do right, and be a friend of men, who shall call it in question and see that there is no evidence for it, help his neighbours to see as he does, and even, if need be, go into the holy tent and break the medicine.

The rule which should guide us in such cases is simple and obvious enough: that the aggregate testimony of our neighbours is subject to the same conditions as the testimony of any one of them.   Namely, we have no right to believe a thing true because everybody says so, unless there are good grounds for believing that some one person at least has the means of knowing what is true, and is speaking the truth so far as he knows it.   However many nations and generations of men are brought into the witness-box, they cannot testify to anything which they do not know.   Every man who has accepted the statement from somebody else, without himself testing and verifying it, is out of court; his word is worth nothing at all.   And when we get back at last to the true birth and beginning of the statement, two serious questions must be disposed of in regard to him who first made it: was he mistaken in thinking that he *knew* about this matter, or was he lying?

This last question is unfortunately a very actual and practical one even to us at this day and in this country. We have no occasion to go to La Salette, or to Central Africa, or to Lourdes, for examples of immoral and debasing superstition. It is only too possible for a child to grow up in London surrounded by an atmosphere of beliefs fit only for the savage, which have in our own time been founded in fraud and propagated by credulity.

Laying aside, then, such tradition as is handed on without testing by successive generations, let us consider that which is truly built up out of the common experience of mankind. This great fabric is for the guidance of our thoughts, and through them of our actions, both in the moral and in the material world. In the moral world, for example, it gives us the conceptions of right in general, of justice, of truth, of beneficence, and the like. These are given as conceptions, not as statements or propositions; they answer to certain definite instincts, which are certainly within us, however they came there. That it is right to be beneficent is matter of immediate personal experience; for when a man retires within himself and there finds something, wider and more lasting than his solitary personality, which says, 'I want to do right,' as well as, 'I want to do good to man,' he can verify by direct observation that one instinct is founded upon and agrees fully with the other. And it is his duty so to verify this and all similar statements.

The tradition says also, at a definite place and time, that such and such actions are just, or true, or beneficent. For all such rules a further inquiry is necessary, since they are sometimes established by an authority other than that of the moral sense founded on experience. Until recently, the moral tradition of our own country—and indeed of all Europe—taught that it was beneficent to give money indiscriminately to beggars. But the questioning of this rule, and investigation into it, led men to see that true beneficence is that which helps a man to do the work which he is most fitted for, not that which keeps and encourages him in idleness; and that to neglect this distinction in the present is to prepare pauperism and misery for the future. By this testing and discussion, not only has practice been purified and made more beneficent, but the very conception of beneficence has been made wider and wiser. Now here the great social heirloom consists of two parts: the instinct of beneficence, which makes a certain side of our nature, when predominant, wish to do good to men; and the intellectual conception of beneficence, which we can compare with any proposed course of conduct and ask, 'Is this beneficent or not?' By the continual asking and answering of such questions the conception grows in breadth and distinctness, and the instinct becomes strengthened and purified. It appears then that the great use of the conception, the intellectual part of the heirloom, is to enable us to ask questions; that it grows and is kept straight by means of these questions; and if we do not use it for that purpose we shall gradually lose it altogether, and be left with a mere code of regulations which cannot rightly be called morality at all.

Such considerations apply even more obviously and clearly, if possible, to the store of beliefs and conceptions which our fathers have amassed for us in respect of the material world. We are ready to laugh at the rule of thumb of the Australian, who continues to tie his hatchet to the side of the handle, although the Birmingham fitter has made a hole on purpose for him to put the handle in. His people have tied up hatchets so for ages: who is he that he should set himself up against their wisdom? He has sunk so low that he cannot do what some of them must have done in the far distant past—call in question an established usage, and invent or learn something better. Yet here, in the dim beginning of knowledge, where science and art are one, we find only the same simple rule which applies to the highest and deepest growths of that cosmic Tree; to its loftiest flower-tipped branches as well as to the profoundest of its hidden roots; the rule, namely, that what is stored up and handed down to us is rightly used by those who act as the makers acted, when they stored it up; those who use it to ask further questions, to examine, to investigate; who try honestly and solemnly to find out what is the right way of looking at things and of dealing with them.

A question rightly asked is already half answered, said Jacobi; we may add that the method of solution is the other half of the answer, and that the actual result counts for nothing by the side of these two. For an example let us go to the telegraph, where theory and practice, grown each to years of discretion, are marvellously wedded for the fruitful service of men. Ohm found that the strength of an electric current is directly proportional to the strength of the battery which produces it, and inversely as the length of the wire along which it has to travel. This is called Ohm's law; but the result, regarded as a statement to be believed, is not the valuable part of it. The first half is the question: what relation holds good between these quantities? So put, the question involves already the conception of strength of current, and of strength of battery, as quantities to be measured and compared; it hints clearly that these are the things to be attended to in the study of electric currents.

The second half is the method of investigation; how to measure these quantities, what instruments are required for the experiment, and how are they to be used? The student who begins to learn about electricity is not asked to believe in Ohm's law: he is made to understand the question, he is placed before the apparatus, and he is taught to verify it. He learns to do things, not to think he knows things; to use instruments and to ask questions, not to accept a traditional statement. The question which required a genius to ask it rightly is answered by a tiro. If Ohm's law were suddenly lost and forgotten by all men, while the question and the method of solution remained, the result could be rediscovered in an hour. But the result by itself, if known to a people who could not comprehend the value of the question or the means of solving it, would be like a watch in the hands of a savage who could not wind it up, or an iron steamship worked by Spanish engineers.[1]

---

[1] A letter of Sunday, July 2, 1876, by Clifford to Lady Pollock, printed in Clifford's *Lectures and Essays*, Vol. I, p. 54-58, may throw some light on Clifford's remarks. Here is an excerpt:

> To-morrow we go by a Spanish boat to Almeira, and thence by diligence or another boat to Malaga. The Spanish boat will be nasty, but it is only twelve hours or so. I am very much better, and shall be glad of a rest at Granada after this gadding about.
>
> P.S. ...
>
> We have seen the Spanish boat, which is called *La Encarnacion*, and that rightly; for it is the incarnation of everything bad.

An editor (probably F. Pollock) commented:

> The *Encarnacion* aforesaid more than justified the worst expectations: the engines broke down at sea, nobody on board was competent to repair them, and the ship lay helpless till a vessel was hailed which had a French engineer on board.

—*AJB*

In regard, then, to the sacred tradition of humanity, we learn that it consists, not in propositions or statements which are to be accepted and believed on the authority of the tradition, but in questions rightly asked, in conceptions which enable us to ask further questions, and in methods of answering questions. The value of all these things depends on their being tested day by day. The very sacredness of the precious deposit imposes upon us the duty and the responsibility of testing it, of purifying and enlarging it to the utmost of our power. He who makes use of its results to stifle his own doubts, or to hamper the inquiry of others, is guilty of a sacrilege which centuries shall never be able to blot out. When the labours and questionings of honest and brave men shall have built up the fabric of known truth to a glory which we in this generation can neither hope for nor imagine, in that pure and holy temple he shall have no part nor lot, but his name and his works shall be cast out into the darkness of oblivion for ever.

III.—The Limits of Inference.

The question in what cases we may believe that which goes beyond our experience, is a very large and delicate one, extending to the whole range of scientific method, and requiring a considerable increase in the application of it before it can be answered with anything approaching to completeness. But one rule, lying on the threshold of the subject, of extreme simplicity and vast practical importance, may here be touched upon and shortly laid down.

A little reflection will show us that every belief, even the simplest and most fundamental, goes beyond experience when regarded as a guide to our actions. A burnt child dreads the fire, because it believes that the fire will burn it to-day just as it did yesterday; but this belief goes beyond experience, and assumes that the unknown fire of to-day is like the known fire of yesterday. Even the belief that the child was burnt yesterday goes beyond *present* experience, which contains only the memory of a burning, and not the burning itself; it assumes, therefore, that this memory is trustworthy, although we know that a memory may often be mistaken. But if it is to be used as a guide to action, as a hint of what the future is to be, it must assume something about that future, namely, that it will be consistent with the supposition that the burning really took place yesterday; which is going beyond experience. Even the fundamental 'I am,' which cannot be doubted, is no guide to action until it takes to itself 'I shall be,' which goes beyond experience. The question is not, therefore, 'May we believe what goes beyond experience?' for this is involved in the very nature of belief; but 'How far and in what manner may we add to our experience in forming our beliefs?'

And an answer, of utter simplicity and universality, is suggested by the example we have taken: a burnt child dreads the fire. We may go beyond experience by assuming that what we do not know is like what we do know; or, in other words, we may add to our experience on the assumption of a uniformity in nature. What this uniformity precisely is, how we grow in the knowledge of it from generation to generation, these are questions which for the present we lay aside, being content to examine two instances which may serve to make plainer the nature of the rule.

From certain observations made with the spectroscope, we infer the existence of hydrogen in the sun. By looking into the spectroscope when the sun is shining on its slit, we see certain definite bright lines: and experiments made upon bodies on the earth have taught us that when these bright lines are seen hydrogen is the source of them. We assume, then, that the unknown bright lines in the sun are like the known bright lines of the laboratory, and that hydrogen in the sun behaves as hydrogen under similar circumstances would behave on the earth.

But are we not trusting our spectroscope too much? Surely, having found it to be trustworthy for terrestrial substances, where its statements can be verified by man, we are justified in accepting its testimony in other like cases; but not when it gives us information about things in the sun, where its testimony cannot be directly verified by man?

Certainly, we want to know a little more before this inference can be justified; and fortunately we do know this. The spectroscope testifies to exactly the same thing in the two cases; namely, that light-vibrations of a certain rate are being sent through it. Its construction is such that if it were wrong about this in one case, it would be wrong in the other. When we come to look into the matter, we find that we have really assumed the matter of the sun to be like the matter of the earth, made up of a certain number of distinct substances; and that each of these, when very hot, has a distinct rate of vibration, by which it may be recognised and singled out from the rest. But this is the kind of assumption which we are justified in using when we add to our experience. It is an assumption of uniformity in nature, and can only be checked by comparison with many similar assumptions which we have to make in other such cases.

But is this a true belief, of the existence of hydrogen in the sun? Can it help in the right guidance of human action?

Certainly not, if it is accepted on unworthy grounds, and without some understanding of the process by which it is got at. But when this process is taken in as the ground of the belief, it becomes a very serious and practical matter. For if there is no hydrogen in the sun, the spectroscope—that is to say, the measurement of rates of vibration—must be an uncertain guide in recognising different substances; and consequently it ought not to be used in chemical analysis—in assaying, for example—to the great saving of time, trouble, and money. Whereas the acceptance of the spectroscopic method as trustworthy has enriched us not only with new metals, which is a great thing, but with new processes of investigation, which is vastly greater.

For another example, let us consider the way in which we infer the truth of an historical event—say the siege of Syracuse in the Peloponnesian war. Our experience is that manuscripts exist which are said to be and which call themselves manuscripts of the history of Thucydides; that in other manuscripts, stated to be by later historians, he is described as living during the time of the war; and that books, supposed to date from the revival of learning, tell us how these manuscripts had been preserved and were then acquired. We find also that men do not, as a rule, forge books and histories without a special motive; we assume that in this respect men in the past were like men in the present; and we observe that in this case no special motive was present. That is, we add to our experience on the assumption of a uniformity in the characters of men. Because our knowledge of this uniformity is far less complete and exact than our knowledge of that which obtains in physics, inferences of the historical kind are more precarious and less exact than inferences in many other sciences.

But if there is any special reason to suspect the character of the persons who wrote or transmitted certain books, the case becomes altered. If a group of documents give internal evidence that they were produced among people who forged books in the names of others, and who, in describing events, suppressed those things which did not suit them, while they amplified such as did suit them; who not only committed these crimes, but gloried in them as proofs of humility and zeal; then we must say that upon such documents no true historical inference can be founded, but only unsatisfactory conjecture.

We may, then, add to our experience on the assumption of a uniformity in nature; we may fill in our picture of what is and has been, as experience gives it us, in such a way as to make the whole consistent with this uniformity. And practically demonstrative inference—that which gives us a right to believe in the result of it—is a clear showing that in no other way than by the truth of this result can the uniformity of nature be saved.

No evidence, therefore, can justify us in believing the truth of a statement which is contrary to, or outside of, the uniformity of nature. If our experience is such that it cannot be filled up consistently with uniformity, all we have a right to conclude is that there is something wrong somewhere; but the possibility of inference is taken away; we must rest in our experience, and not go beyond it at all. If an event really happened which was not a part of the uniformity of nature, it would have two properties: no evidence could give the right to believe it to any except those whose actual experience it was; and no inference worthy of belief could be founded upon it at all.

Are we then bound to believe that nature is absolutely and universally uniform? Certainly not; we have no right to believe anything of this kind. The rule only tells us that in forming beliefs which go beyond our experience, we may make the assumption that nature is practically uniform so far as we are concerned. Within the range of human action and verification, we may form, by help of this assumption, actual beliefs; beyond it, only those hypotheses which serve for the more accurate asking of questions.

To sum up:—

We may believe what goes beyond our experience, only when it is inferred from that experience by the assumption that what we do not know is like what we know.

We may believe the statement of another person, when there is reasonable ground for supposing that he knows the matter of which he speaks, and that he is speaking the truth so far as he knows it.

It is wrong in all cases to believe on insufficient evidence; and where it is presumption to doubt and to investigate, there it is worse than presumption to believe.

The Will to Believe

1897

William James

THE WILL TO BELIEVE.[1]

IN the recently published Life by Leslie Stephen of his brother, Fitz-James, there is an account of a school to which the latter went when he was a boy. The teacher, a certain Mr. Guest, used to converse with his pupils in this wise: "Gurney, what is the difference between justification and sanctification? — Stephen, prove the omnipotence of God!" etc. In the midst of our Harvard freethinking and indifference we are prone to imagine that here at your good old orthodox College conversation continues to be somewhat upon this order; and to show you that we at Harvard have not lost all interest in these vital subjects, I have brought with me to-night something like a sermon on justification by faith to read to you, — I mean an essay in justification *of* faith, a defence of our right to adopt a believing attitude in religious matters, in spite of the fact that our merely logical intellect may not have been coerced. 'The Will to Believe,' accordingly, is the title of my paper.

---

[1] An Address to the Philosophical Clubs of Yale and Brown Universities. Published in the New World, June, 1896.

I have long defended to my own students the lawfulness of voluntarily adopted faith; but as soon as they have got well imbued with the logical spirit, they have as a rule refused to admit my contention to be lawful philosophically, even though in point of fact they were personally all the time chock-full of some faith or other themselves. I am all the while, however, so profoundly convinced that my own position is correct, that your invitation has seemed to me a good occasion to make my statements more clear. Perhaps your minds will be more open than those with which I have hitherto had to deal. I will be as little technical as I can, though I must begin by setting up some technical distinctions that will help us in the end.

I.

Let us give the name of *hypothesis* to anything that may be proposed to our belief; and just as the electricians speak of live and dead wires, let us speak of any hypothesis as either *live* or *dead*. A live hypothesis is one which appeals as a real possibility to him to whom it is proposed. If I ask you to believe in the Mahdi, the notion makes no electric connection with your nature, — it refuses to scintillate with any credibility at all. As an hypothesis it is completely dead. To an Arab, however (even if he be not one of the Mahdi's followers), the hypothesis is among the mind's possibilities: it is alive. This shows that deadness and liveness in an hypothesis are not intrinsic properties, but relations to the individual thinker. They are measured by his willingness to act. The maximum of liveness in an hypothesis means willingness to act irrevocably.

Practically, that means belief; but there is some believing tendency wherever there is willingness to act at all.

Next, let us call the decision between two hypotheses an *option*. Options may be of several kinds. They may be — 1, *living* or *dead; 2, forced* or *avoidable;* 3, *momentous* or *trivial;* and for our purposes we may call an option a *genuine* option when it is of the forced, living, and momentous kind.

1. A living option is one in which both hypotheses are live ones. If I say to you: "Be a theosophist or be a Mohammedan," it is probably a dead option, because for you neither hypothesis is likely to be alive. But if I say: "Be an agnostic or be a Christian," it is otherwise: trained as you are, each hypothesis makes some appeal, however small, to your belief.

2. Next, if I say to you: "Choose between going out with your umbrella or without it," I do not offer you a genuine option, for it is not forced. You can easily avoid it by not going out at all. Similarly, if I say, "Either love me or hate me," "Either call my theory true or call it false," your option is avoidable. You may remain indifferent to me, neither loving nor hating, and you may decline to offer any judgment as to my theory. But if I say, "Either accept this truth or go without it," I put on you a forced option, for there is no standing place outside of the alternative. Every dilemma based on a complete logical disjunction, with no possibility of not choosing, is an option of this forced kind.

3. Finally, if I were Dr. Nansen and proposed to you to join my North Pole expedition, your option would be momentous; for this would probably be your only similar opportunity, and your choice now would either exclude you from the North Pole sort of immortality altogether or put at least the chance of it into your hands. He who refuses to

embrace a unique opportunity loses the prize as surely as if he tried and failed. *Per contra*, the option is trivial when the opportunity is not unique, when the stake is insignificant, or when the decision is reversible if it later prove unwise. Such trivial options abound in the scientific life. A chemist finds an hypothesis live enough to spend a year in its verification: he believes in it to that extent. But if his experiments prove inconclusive either way, he is quit for his loss of time, no vital harm being done.

It will facilitate our discussion if we keep all these distinctions well in mind.

II.

The next matter to consider is the actual psychology of human opinion. When we look at certain facts, it seems as if our passional and volitional nature lay at the root of all our convictions. When we look at others, it seems as if they could do nothing when the intellect had once said its say. Let us take the latter facts up first.

Does it not seem preposterous on the very face of it to talk of our opinions being modifiable at will? Can our will either help or hinder our intellect in its perceptions of truth? Can we, by just willing it, believe that Abraham Lincoln's existence is a myth, and that the portraits of him in McClure's Magazine are all of some one else? Can we, by any effort of our will, or by any strength of wish that it were true, believe ourselves well and about when we are roaring with rheumatism in bed, or feel certain that the sum of the two one-dollar bills in our pocket must be a hundred dollars? We can *say* any of these things, but we are absolutely impotent to believe them; and of just such things is the whole fabric of the truths that we do believe in made up, — matters of fact, immediate or remote, as Hume said, and relations between ideas, which are either there or not there for us if we see them so, and which if not there cannot be put there by any action of our own.

In Pascal's Thoughts there is a celebrated passage known in literature as Pascal's wager. In it he tries to force us into Christianity by reasoning as if our concern with truth resembled our concern with the stakes in a game of chance. Translated freely his words are these: You must either believe or not believe that God is — which will you do? Your human reason cannot say. A game is going on between you and the nature of things which at the day of judgment will bring out either heads or tails. Weigh what your gains and your losses would be if you should stake all you have on heads, or God's existence: if you win in such case, you gain eternal beatitude; if you lose, you lose nothing at all. If there were an infinity of chances, and only one for God in this wager, still you ought to stake your all on God; for though you surely risk a finite loss by this procedure, any finite loss is reasonable, even a certain one is reasonable, if there is but the possibility of infinite gain. Go, then, and take holy water, and have masses said; belief will come and stupefy your scruples, — *Cela vous fera croire et vous abêtira.* Why should you not? At bottom, what have you to lose?

You probably feel that when religious faith expresses itself thus, in the language of the gaming-table, it is put to its last trumps. Surely Pascal's own personal belief in masses and holy water had far other springs; and this celebrated page of his is but an argument for others, a last desperate snatch at a weapon against the hardness of the unbelieving heart. We feel that a faith in masses and holy water adopted wilfully after such a mechanical calculation would lack the inner soul of faith's reality; and if we were ourselves in the place of the Deity, we should probably take particular pleasure in cutting off believers of this pattern from their infinite reward. It is evident that unless there be some pre-existing tendency to believe in masses and holy water, the option offered to the will by Pascal is not a living option. Certainly no Turk ever took to masses and holy water on its account; and even to us Protestants these means of salvation seem such foregone impossibilities that Pascal's logic, invoked for them specifically, leaves us unmoved. As well might the Mahdi write to us, saying, "I am the Expected One whom God has created in his effulgence. You shall be infinitely happy if you confess me; otherwise you shall be cut off from the light of the sun. Weigh, then, your infinite gain if I am genuine against your finite sacrifice if I am not!" His logic would be that of Pascal; but he would vainly use it on us, for the hypothesis he offers us is dead. No tendency to act on it exists in us to any degree.

The talk of believing by our volition seems, then, from one point of view, simply silly. From another point of view it is worse than silly, it is vile. When one turns to the magnificent edifice of the physical sciences, and sees how it was reared; what thousands of disinterested moral lives of men lie buried in its mere foundations; what patience and postponement, what choking down of preference, what submission to the icy laws of outer fact are wrought into its very stones and mortar; how absolutely impersonal it stands in its vast augustness, — then how besotted and contemptible seems every little sentimentalist who comes blowing his voluntary smoke-wreaths, and pretending to decide things from out of his private dream! Can we wonder if those bred in the rugged and manly school of science should feel like spewing such subjectivism out of their mouths? The whole system of loyalties which grow up in the schools of science go dead against its toleration; so that it is only natural that those who have caught the scientific fever should pass over to the opposite extreme, and write sometimes as if the incorruptibly truthful intellect ought positively to prefer bitterness and unacceptableness to the heart in its cup.

> It fortifies my soul to know
> That, though I perish, Truth is so —

sings Clough, while Huxley exclaims: "My only consolation lies in the reflection that, however bad our posterity may become, so far as they hold by the plain rule of not pretending to believe what they have no reason to believe, because it may be to their advantage so to pretend [the word 'pretend' is surely here redundant], they will not have reached the lowest depth of immorality." And that delicious *enfant terrible* Clifford writes: "Belief is desecrated when given to unproved and unquestioned statements for the solace and private pleasure of the believer. . . . Whoso would deserve well of his fellows in this matter will guard the purity of his belief with a very fanaticism of jealous care, lest at any time it should rest on an unworthy object, and catch a stain which can never be wiped away. . . . If [a] belief has been accepted on insufficient evidence [even though the belief be true, as Clifford on the same page explains] the pleasure is a stolen one. . . . It is sinful because it is stolen in defiance of our duty to mankind. That duty is to guard ourselves from such beliefs as from a pestilence which may shortly master our own body and then spread to the rest of the town. . . . It is

wrong always, everywhere, and for every one, to believe
anything upon insufficient evidence."

III.

All this strikes one as healthy, even when expressed, as
by Clifford, with somewhat too much of robustious pathos
in the voice. Free-will and simple wishing do seem, in the
matter of our credences, to be only fifth wheels to the
coach. Yet if any one should thereupon assume that
intellectual insight is what remains after wish and will and
sentimental preference have taken wing, or that pure reason
is what then settles our opinions, he would fly quite as
directly in the teeth of the facts.

It is only our already dead hypotheses that our willing
nature is unable to bring to life again. But what has made
them dead for us is for the most part a previous action of
our willing nature of an antagonistic kind. When I say
'willing nature,' I do not mean only such deliberate
volitions as may have set up habits of belief that we cannot
now escape from, — I mean all such factors of belief as
fear and hope, prejudice and passion, imitation and
partisanship, the circumpressure of our caste and set. As a
matter of fact we find ourselves believing, we hardly know
how or why. Mr. Balfour gives the name of 'authority' to
all those influences, born of the intellectual climate, that
make hypotheses possible or impossible for us, alive or
dead. Here in this room, we all of us believe in molecules
and the conservation of energy, in democracy and necessary
progress, in Protestant Christianity and the duty of fighting
for 'the doctrine of the immortal Monroe,' all for no
reasons worthy of the name. We see into these matters

with no more inner clearness, and probably with much less, than any disbeliever in them might possess. His unconventionality would probably have some grounds to show for its conclusions; but for us, not insight, but the *prestige* of the opinions, is what makes the spark shoot from them and light up our sleeping magazines of faith. Our reason is quite satisfied, in nine hundred and ninety-nine cases out of every thousand of us, if it can find a few arguments that will do to recite in case our credulity is criticized by some one else. Our faith is faith in some one else's faith, and in the greatest matters this is most the case. Our belief in truth itself, for instance, that there is a truth, and that our minds and it are made for each other, — what is it but a passionate affirmation of desire, in which our social system backs us up? We want to have a truth; we want to believe that our experiments and studies and discussions must put us in a continually better and better position towards it; and on this line we agree to fight out our thinking lives. But if a pyrrhonistic sceptic asks us *how we know* all this, can our logic find a reply? No! certainly it cannot. It is just one volition against another, — we willing to go in for life upon a trust or assumption which he, for his part, does not care to make.[1]

As a rule we disbelieve all facts and theories for which we have no use. Clifford's cosmic emotions find no use for Christian feelings. Huxley belabors the bishops because there is no use for sacerdotalism in his scheme of life. Newman, on the contrary, goes over to Romanism, and finds all sorts of reasons good for staying there, because a priestly system is for him an organic need and delight.

---

[1] Compare the admirable page 310 in S. H. Hodgson's "Time and Space," London, 1865.

Why do so few 'scientists' even look at the evidence for telepathy, so called?   Because they think, as a leading biologist, now dead, once said to me, that even if such a thing were true, scientists ought to band together to keep it suppressed and concealed. It would undo the uniformity of Nature and all sorts of other things without which scientists cannot carry on their pursuits. But if this very man had been shown something which as a scientist he might *do* with telepathy, he might not only have examined the evidence, but even have found it good enough. This very law which the logicians would impose upon us — if I may give the name of logicians to those who would rule out our willing nature here — is based on nothing but their own natural wish to exclude all elements for which they, in their professional quality of logicians, can find no use.

Evidently, then, our non-intellectual nature does influence our convictions. There are passional tendencies and volitions which run before and others which come after belief, and it is only the latter that are too late for the fair; and they are not too late when the previous passional work has been already in their own direction. Pascal's argument, instead of being powerless, then seems a regular clincher, and is the last stroke needed to make our faith in masses and holy water complete. The state of things is evidently far from simple; and pure insight and logic, whatever they might do ideally, are not the only things that really do produce our creeds.

IV.

Our next duty, having recognized this mixed-up state of affairs, is to ask whether it be simply reprehensible and pathological, or whether, on the contrary, we must treat it as a normal element in making up our minds. The thesis I defend is, briefly stated, this: *Our passional nature not only lawfully may, but must, decide an option between propositions, whenever it is a genuine option that cannot by its nature be decided on intellectual grounds; for to say, under such circumstances, "Do not decide, but leave the question open," is itself a passional decision, — just like deciding yes or no, — and is attended with the same risk of losing the truth.* The thesis thus abstractly expressed will, I trust, soon become quite clear. But I must first indulge in a bit more of preliminary work.

V.

It will be observed that for the purposes of this discussion we are on 'dogmatic' ground, — ground, I mean, which leaves systematic philosophical scepticism altogether out of account. The postulate that there is truth, and that it is the destiny of our minds to attain it, we are deliberately resolving to make, though the sceptic will not make it. We part company with him, therefore, absolutely, at this point. But the faith that truth exists, and that our minds can find it, may be held in two ways. We may talk of the *empiricist* way and of the *absolutist* way of believing in truth. The absolutists in this matter say that we not only can attain to knowing truth, but we can *know when* we have attained to knowing it; while the empiricists think that although we may attain it, we cannot infallibly know when. To *know* is one thing, and to know for certain *that* we know is another. One may hold to the first being possible without the second; hence the empiricists and the absolutists, although neither of them is a sceptic in the usual philosophic sense of the term, show very different degrees of dogmatism in their lives.

If we look at the history of opinions, we see that the empiricist tendency has largely prevailed in science, while in philosophy the absolutist tendency has had everything its own way. The characteristic sort of happiness, indeed, which philosophies yield has mainly consisted in the conviction felt by each successive school or system that by it bottom-certitude had been attained. "Other philosophies are collections of opinions, mostly false; *my* philosophy gives standing-ground forever," — who does not recognize in this the key-note of every system worthy of the name? A system, to be a system at all, must come as a *closed* system, reversible in this or that detail, perchance, but in its essential features never!

Scholastic orthodoxy, to which one must always go when one wishes to find perfectly clear statement, has beautifully elaborated this absolutist conviction in a doctrine which it calls that of 'objective evidence.' If, for example, I am unable to doubt that I now exist before you, that two is less than three, or that if all men are mortal then I am mortal too, it is because these things illumine my intellect irresistibly. The final ground of this objective evidence possessed by certain propositions is the *adæquatio intellectûs nostri cum rê*. The certitude it brings involves an *aptitudinem ad extorquendum certum assensum* on the part of the truth envisaged, and on the side of the subject a *quietem in cognitione*, when once the object is mentally received, that leaves no possibility of doubt behind; and in the whole transaction nothing operates but the *entitas ipsa* of the object and the *entitas ipsa* of the mind. We slouchy modern thinkers dislike to talk in Latin, — indeed, we dislike to talk in set terms at all; but at bottom our own state of mind is very much like this whenever we uncritically abandon ourselves: You believe in objective evidence, and I do. Of some things we feel that we are certain: we know, and we know that we do know. There is something that gives a click inside of us, a bell that strikes twelve, when the hands of our mental clock have swept the dial and meet over the meridian hour. The greatest empiricists among us are only empiricists on reflection: when left to their instincts, they dogmatize like infallible popes. When the Cliffords tell us how sinful it is to be Christians on such 'insufficient evidence,' insufficiency is really the last thing they have in mind. For them the evidence is absolutely sufficient, only it makes the other way. They believe so completely in an anti-christian order of the universe that there is no living option: Christianity is a dead hypothesis from the start.

VI.

But now, since we are all such absolutists by instinct, what in our quality of students of philosophy ought we to do about the fact? Shall we espouse and indorse it? Or shall we treat it as a weakness of our nature from which we must free ourselves, if we can?

I sincerely believe that the latter course is the only one we can follow as reflective men. Objective evidence and certitude are doubtless very fine ideals to play with, but where on this moonlit and dream-visited planet are they found? I am, therefore, myself a complete empiricist so far as my theory of human knowledge goes. I live, to be sure, by the practical faith that we must go on experiencing and thinking over our experience, for only thus can our opinions grow more true; but to hold any one of them — I absolutely do not care which — as if it never could be reinterpretable or corrigible, I believe to be a tremendously mistaken attitude, and I think that the whole history of philosophy will bear me out.   There is but one indefectibly certain truth, and that is the truth that pyrrhonistic scepticism itself leaves standing, — the truth that the present phenomenon of consciousness exists.   That, however, is the bare starting-point of knowledge, the mere admission of a stuff to be philosophized about.   The various philosophies are but so many attempts at expressing what this stuff really is.   And if we repair to our libraries what disagreement do we discover!   Where is a certainly true answer found?   Apart from abstract propositions of comparison (such as two and two are the same as four), propositions which tell us nothing by themselves about concrete reality, we find no proposition ever regarded by any one as evidently certain that has not either been called a falsehood, or at least had its truth sincerely questioned by some one else.   The transcending of the axioms of geometry, not in play but in earnest, by certain of our contemporaries (as Zöllner and Charles H. Hinton), and the rejection of the whole Aristotelian logic by the Hegelians, are striking instances in point.

No concrete test of what is really true has ever been agreed upon.   Some make the criterion external to the moment of perception, putting it either in revelation, the *consensus gentium*, the instincts of the heart, or the systematized experience of the race.   Others make the perceptive moment its own test, — Descartes, for instance, with his clear and distinct ideas guaranteed by the veracity of God; Reid with his 'common-sense;' and Kant with his forms of synthetic judgment *a priori*. The inconceivability of the opposite; the capacity to be verified by sense; the possession of complete organic unity or self-relation, realized when a thing is its own other, — are standards which, in turn, have been used. The much lauded objective evidence is never triumphantly there; it is a mere aspiration or *Grenzbegriff*, marking the infinitely remote ideal of our thinking life. To claim that certain truths now possess it, is simply to say that when you think them true and they *are* true, then their evidence is objective, otherwise it is not. But practically one's conviction that the evidence one goes by is of the real objective brand, is only one more subjective opinion added to the lot. For what a contradictory array of opinions have objective evidence and absolute certitude been claimed! The world is rational through and through, — its existence is an ultimate brute fact; there is a personal God, — a personal God is inconceivable; there is an extra-mental physical world immediately known, — the mind can only know its own ideas; a moral imperative exists, — obligation is only the resultant of desires; a permanent spiritual principle is in every one, — there are only shifting states of mind; there is an endless chain of causes, — there is an absolute first cause; an eternal necessity, — a freedom; a purpose, — no purpose; a primal One, — a primal Many; a universal continuity, — an essential discontinuity in things; an infinity, — no infinity. There is this, — there is that; there is indeed nothing which some one has not thought absolutely true, while his neighbor deemed it absolutely false; and not an absolutist among them seems ever to have considered that the trouble may all the time be essential, and that the intellect, even with truth directly in its grasp, may have no infallible signal for knowing whether it be truth or no. When, indeed, one remembers that the most striking practical application to life of the doctrine of objective certitude has been the conscientious labors of the Holy Office of the Inquisition, one feels less tempted than ever to lend the doctrine a respectful ear.

But please observe, now, that when as empiricists we give up the doctrine of objective certitude, we do not thereby give up the quest or hope of truth itself. We still pin our faith on its existence, and still believe that we gain an ever better position towards it by systematically continuing to roll up experiences and think. Our great difference from the scholastic lies in the way we face. The strength of his system lies in the principles, the origin, the *terminus a quo* of his thought; for us the strength is in the outcome, the upshot, the *terminus ad quem*. Not where it comes from but what it leads to is to decide. It matters not to an empiricist from what quarter an hypothesis may come to him: he may have acquired it by fair means or by foul; passion may have whispered or accident suggested it; but if the total drift of thinking continues to confirm it, that is what he means by its being true.

VII.

One more point, small but important, and our preliminaries are done. There are two ways of looking at our duty in the matter of opinion, — ways entirely different, and yet ways about whose difference the theory of knowledge seems hitherto to have shown very little concern. *We must know the truth;* and *we must avoid error*, — these are our first and great commandments as would-be knowers; but they are not two ways of stating an identical commandment, they are two separable laws. Although it may indeed happen that when we believe the truth *A*, we escape as an incidental consequence from believing the falsehood *B*, it hardly ever happens that by merely disbelieving *B* we necessarily believe *A*. We may in escaping *B* fall into believing other falsehoods, *C* or *D*, just as bad as *B*; or we may escape *B* by not believing anything at all, not even *A*.

Believe truth! Shun error! — these, we see, are two materially different laws; and by choosing between them we may end,[1] coloring differently our whole intellectual life. We may regard the chase for truth as paramount, and the avoidance of error as secondary; or we may, on the other hand, treat the avoidance of error as more imperative, and let truth take its chance. Clifford, in the instructive passage which I have quoted, exhorts us to the latter course. Believe nothing, he tells us, keep your mind in suspense forever, rather than by closing it on insufficient evidence incur the awful risk of believing lies. You, on the other hand, may think that the risk of being in error is a very small matter when compared with the blessings of real knowledge, and be ready to be duped many times in your investigation rather than postpone indefinitely the chance of guessing true. I myself find it impossible to go with Clifford. We must remember that these feelings of our duty about either truth or error are in any case only expressions of our passional life. Biologically considered, our minds are as ready to grind out falsehood as veracity, and he who says, "Better go without belief forever than believe a lie!"

---

[1] In the 1897 edition, a comma appears after the word "end"; in all of the subsequent editions that I have seen, the comma is removed and the word "by" appears in its place. —*AJB*

merely shows his own preponderant private horror of becoming a dupe. He may be critical of many of his desires and fears, but this fear he slavishly obeys. He cannot imagine any one questioning its binding force. For my own part, I have also a horror of being duped; but I can believe that worse things than being duped may happen to a man in this world: so Clifford's exhortation has to my ears a thoroughly fantastic sound. It is like a general informing his soldiers that it is better to keep out of battle forever than to risk a single wound. Not so are victories either over enemies or over nature gained. Our errors are surely not such awfully solemn things. In a world where we are so certain to incur them in spite of all our caution, a certain lightness of heart seems healthier than this excessive nervousness on their behalf. At any rate, it seems the fittest thing for the empiricist philosopher.

VIII.

And now, after all this introduction, let us go straight at our question. I have said, and now repeat it, that not only as a matter of fact do we find our passional nature influencing us in our opinions, but that there are some options between opinions in which this influence must be regarded both as an inevitable and as a lawful determinant of our choice.

I fear here that some of you my hearers will begin to scent danger, and lend an inhospitable ear. Two first steps of passion you have indeed had to admit as necessary, — we must think so as to avoid dupery, and we must think so as to gain truth; but the surest path to those ideal consummations, you will probably consider, is from now onwards to take no further passional step.

Well, of course, I agree as far as the facts will allow. Wherever the option between losing truth and gaining it is not momentous, we can throw the chance of *gaining truth* away, and at any rate save ourselves from any chance of *believing falsehood*, by not making up our minds at all till objective evidence has come. In scientific questions, this is almost always the case; and even in human affairs in general, the need of acting is seldom so urgent that a false belief to act on is better than no belief at all. Law courts, indeed, have to decide on the best evidence attainable for the moment, because a judge's duty is to make law as well as to ascertain it, and (as a learned judge once said to me) few cases are worth spending much time over: the great thing is to have them decided on *any* acceptable principle, and got out of the way. But in our dealings with objective nature we obviously are recorders, not makers, of the truth; and decisions for the mere sake of deciding promptly and getting on to the next business would be wholly out of place. Throughout the breadth of physical nature facts are what they are quite independently of us, and seldom is there any such hurry about them that the risks of being duped by believing a premature theory need be faced. The questions here are always trivial options, the hypotheses are hardly living (at any rate not living for us spectators), the choice between believing truth or falsehood is seldom forced. The attitude of sceptical balance is therefore the absolutely wise one if we would escape mistakes. What difference, indeed, does it make to most of us whether we have or have not a theory of the Röntgen rays,[1] whether we believe or not in mind-stuff, or have a conviction about the causality of

---

[1] Wilhelm Röntgen is the German physicist who, in 1895, discovered X-rays, which were called "Röntgen rays." —*AJB*

conscious states? It makes no difference. Such options are not forced on us. On every account it is better not to make them, but still keep weighing reasons *pro et contra* with an indifferent hand.

I speak, of course, here of the purely judging mind. For purposes of discovery such indifference is to be less highly recommended, and science would be far less advanced than she is if the passionate desires of individuals to get their own faiths confirmed had been kept out of the game. See for example the sagacity which Spencer and Weismann now display. On the other hand, if you want an absolute duffer in an investigation, you must, after all, take the man who has no interest whatever in its results: he is the warranted incapable, the positive fool. The most useful investigator, because the most sensitive observer, is always he whose eager interest in one side of the question is balanced by an equally keen nervousness lest he become deceived.[1] Science has organized this nervousness into a regular *technique*, her so-called method of verification; and she has fallen so deeply in love with the method that one may even say she has ceased to care for truth by itself at all. It is only truth as technically verified that interests her. The truth of truths might come in merely affirmative form, and she would decline to touch it. Such truth as that, she might repeat with Clifford, would be stolen in defiance of her duty to mankind. Human passions, however, are stronger than technical rules. "Le cœur a ses raisons," as Pascal says, "que la raison ne connaît pas;" and however indifferent to all but the bare rules of the game the umpire, the abstract intellect, may be, the concrete players who furnish him the

[1] Compare Wilfrid Ward's Essay, "The Wish to Believe," in his *Witnesses to the Unseen*, Macmillan & Co., 1893.

materials to judge of are usually, each one of them, in love with some pet 'live hypothesis' of his own. Let us agree, however, that wherever there is no forced option, the dispassionately judicial intellect with no pet hypothesis, saving us, as it does, from dupery at any rate, ought to be our ideal.

The question next arises: Are there not somewhere forced options in our speculative questions, and can we (as men who may be interested at least as much in positively gaining truth as in merely escaping dupery) always wait with impunity till the coercive evidence shall have arrived? It seems *a priori* improbable that the truth should be so nicely adjusted to our needs and powers as that. In the great boarding-house of nature, the cakes and the butter and the syrup seldom come out so even and leave the plates so clean. Indeed, we should view them with scientific suspicion if they did.

IX.

Moral questions immediately present themselves as questions whose solution cannot wait for sensible proof. A moral question is a question not of what sensibly exists, but of what is good, or would be good if it did exist. Science can tell us what exists; but to compare the *worths*, both of what exists and of what does not exist, we must consult not science, but what Pascal calls our heart. Science herself consults her heart when she lays it down that the infinite ascertainment of fact and correction of false belief are the supreme goods for man. Challenge the statement, and science can only repeat it oracularly, or else prove it by showing that such ascertainment and correction bring man all sorts of other goods which man's heart in turn declares. The question of having moral beliefs at all or not having them is decided by our will. Are our moral preferences true or false, or are they only odd biological phenomena, making things good or bad for *us*, but in themselves indifferent? How can your pure intellect decide? If your heart does not *want* a world of moral reality, your head will assuredly never make you believe in one. Mephistophelian scepticism, indeed, will satisfy the head's play-instincts much better than any rigorous idealism can. Some men (even at the student age) are so naturally cool-hearted that the moralistic hypothesis never has for them any pungent life, and in their supercilious presence the hot young moralist always feels strangely ill at ease. The appearance of knowingness is on their side, of *naïveté* and gullibility on his. Yet, in the inarticulate heart of him, he clings to it that he is not a dupe, and that there is a realm in which (as Emerson says) all their wit and intellectual superiority is no better than the cunning of a fox. Moral scepticism can no more be refuted or proved by logic than intellectual scepticism can. When we stick to it that there *is* truth (be it of either kind), we do so with our whole nature, and resolve to stand or fall by the results. The sceptic with his whole nature adopts the doubting attitude; but which of us is the wiser, Omniscience only knows.

Turn now from these wide questions of good to a certain class of questions of fact, questions concerning personal relations, states of mind between one man and another. *Do you like me or not?* — for example. Whether you do or not depends, in countless instances, on whether I meet you half-way, am willing to assume that you must like me, and show you trust and expectation. The previous faith on my part in your liking's existence is in such cases what makes your liking come. But if I stand aloof, and refuse to budge an inch until I have objective evidence, until you shall have done something apt, as the absolutists say, *ad extorquendum assensum meum*, ten to one your liking never comes.   How many women's hearts are vanquished by the mere sanguine insistence of some man that they *must* love him! he will not consent to the hypothesis that they cannot.   The desire for a certain kind of truth here brings about that special truth's existence; and so it is in innumerable cases of other sorts.   Who gains promotions, boons, appointments, but the man in whose life they are seen to play the part of live hypotheses, who discounts them, sacrifices other things for their sake before they have come, and takes risks for them in advance?   His faith acts on the powers above him as a claim, and creates its own verification.

A social organism of any sort whatever, large or small, is what it is because each member proceeds to his own duty with a trust that the other members will simultaneously do theirs.   Wherever a desired result is achieved by the co-operation of many independent persons, its existence as a fact is a pure consequence of the precursive faith in one another of those immediately concerned. A government, an army, a commercial system, a ship, a college, an athletic team, all exist on this condition, without which not only is nothing achieved, but nothing is even attempted. A whole train of passengers (individually brave enough) will be looted by a few highwaymen, simply because the latter can count on one another, while each passenger fears that if he makes a movement of resistance, he will be shot before any one else backs him up. If we believed that the whole car-full would rise at once with us, we should each severally rise, and train-robbing would never even be attempted.

There are, then, cases where a fact cannot come at all unless a preliminary faith exists in its coming. *And where faith in a fact can help create the fact*, that would be an insane logic which should say that faith running ahead of scientific evidence is the 'lowest kind of immorality' into which a thinking being can fall. Yet such is the logic by which our scientific absolutists pretend to regulate our lives!

X.

In truths dependent on our personal action, then, faith based on desire is certainly a lawful and possibly an indispensable thing.

But now, it will be said, these are all childish human cases, and have nothing to do with great cosmical matters, like the question of religious faith. Let us then pass on to that. Religions differ so much in their accidents that in discussing the religious question we must make it very generic and broad. What then do we now mean by the religious hypothesis? Science says things are; morality says some things are better than other things; and religion says essentially two things.

First, she says that the best things are the more eternal things, the overlapping things, the things in the universe that throw the last stone, so to speak, and say the final word. "Perfection is eternal," — this phrase of Charles Secrétan seems a good way of putting this first affirmation of religion, an affirmation which obviously cannot yet be verified scientifically at all.

The second affirmation of religion is that we are better off even now if we believe her first affirmation to be true.

Now, let us consider what the logical elements of this situation are *in case the religious hypothesis in both its branches be really true.* (Of course, we must admit that possibility at the outset. If we are to discuss the question at all, it must involve a living option. If for any of you religion be a hypothesis that cannot, by any living possibility be true, then you need go no farther. I speak to the 'saving remnant' alone.) So proceeding, we see, first, that religion offers itself as a *momentous* option. We are supposed to gain, even now, by our belief, and to lose by our non-belief, a certain vital good. Secondly, religion is a *forced* option, so far as that good goes. We cannot escape the issue by remaining sceptical and waiting for more light, because, although we do avoid error in that way *if religion be untrue*, we lose the good, *if it be true*, just as certainly as if we positively chose to disbelieve. It is as if a man should hesitate indefinitely to ask a certain woman to marry him because he was not perfectly sure that she would prove an angel after he brought her home. Would he not cut himself off from that particular angel-possibility as decisively as if he went and married some one else? Scepticism, then, is not avoidance of option; it is option of a certain particular kind of risk. *Better risk loss of truth than chance of error,* — that is your faith-vetoer's exact position. He is actively playing his stake as much as the believer is; he is backing the field against the religious hypothesis, just as the believer is backing the religious hypothesis against the field. To preach scepticism to us as a duty until 'sufficient evidence' for religion be found, is tantamount therefore to telling us, when in presence of the religious hypothesis, that to yield to our fear of its being error is wiser and better than to yield to our hope that it may be true. It is not intellect against all passions, then; it is only intellect with one passion laying down its law. And by what, forsooth, is the supreme wisdom of this passion warranted? Dupery for dupery, what proof is there that dupery through hope is so much worse than dupery through fear? I, for one, can see no proof; and I simply refuse obedience to the scientist's command to imitate his kind of option, in a case where my own stake is important enough to give me the right to choose my own form of risk. If religion be true and the evidence for it be still insufficient, I do not wish, by putting your extinguisher upon my nature (which feels to me as if it had after all some business in this matter), to forfeit my sole chance in life of getting upon the winning side, — that chance depending, of course, on my willingness to run the risk of acting as if my passional need of taking the world religiously might be prophetic and right.

All this is on the supposition that it really may be prophetic and right, and that, even to us who are discussing the matter, religion is a live hypothesis which may be true. Now, to most of us religion comes in a still further way that makes a veto on our active faith even more illogical. The more perfect and more eternal aspect of the universe is represented in our religions as having personal form. The universe is no longer a mere *It* to us, but a *Thou*, if we are religious; and any relation that may be possible from person to person might be possible here. For instance, although in one sense we are passive portions of the universe, in another we show a curious autonomy, as if we were small active centres on our own account. We feel, too, as if the appeal of religion to us were made to our own active good-will, as if evidence might be forever withheld from us unless we met the hypothesis half-way. To take a trivial illustration: just as a man who in a company of gentlemen made no advances, asked a warrant for every concession, and believed no one's word without proof, would cut himself off by such churlishness from all the social rewards that a more trusting spirit would earn, — so here, one who should shut himself up in snarling logicality and try to make the gods extort his recognition willy-nilly, or not get it at all, might cut himself off forever from his only opportunity of making the gods' acquaintance. This feeling, forced on us we know not whence, that by obstinately believing that there are gods (although not to do so would be so easy both for our logic and our life) we are doing the universe the deepest service we can, seems part of the living essence of the religious hypothesis. If the hypothesis *were* true in all its parts, including this one, then pure intellectualism, with its veto on our making willing advances, would be an absurdity; and some participation of our sympathetic nature would be logically required. I, therefore, for one, cannot see my way to accepting the agnostic rules for truth-seeking, or wilfully agree to keep my willing nature out of the game. I cannot do so for this plain reason, that *a rule of thinking which would absolutely prevent me from acknowledging certain kinds of truth if those kinds of truth were really there, would be an irrational rule.* That for me is the long and short of the formal logic of the situation, no matter what the kinds of truth might materially be.

I confess I do not see how this logic can be escaped. But sad experience makes me fear that some of you may still shrink from radically saying with me, *in abstracto*, that we have the right to believe at our own risk any hypothesis that is live enough to tempt our will. I suspect, however, that if this is so, it is because you have got away from the abstract logical point of view altogether, and are thinking (perhaps without realizing it) of some particular religious hypothesis which for you is dead. The freedom to 'believe what we will' you apply to the case of some patent superstition; and the faith you think of is the faith defined by the schoolboy when he said, "Faith is when you believe something that you know ain't true." I can only repeat that this is misapprehension. *In concreto*, the freedom to believe can only cover living options which the intellect of the individual cannot by itself resolve; and living options never seem absurdities to him who has them to consider. When I look at the religious question as it really puts itself to concrete men, and when I think of all the possibilities which both practically and theoretically it involves, then this command that we shall put a stopper on our heart, instincts, and courage, and *wait* — acting of course meanwhile more or less as if religion were *not* true[1] — till doomsday, or till such time as our intellect and senses working together may have raked in evidence enough, — this command, I say, seems to me the queerest idol ever manufactured in the philosophic cave. Were we scholastic absolutists, there might be more excuse. If we had an infallible intellect with its objective certitudes, we might feel ourselves disloyal to such a perfect organ of knowledge

---

[1] Since belief is measured by action, he who forbids us to believe religion to be true, necessarily also forbids us to act as we should if we did believe it to be true. The whole defence of religious faith hinges upon action. If the action required or inspired by the religious hypothesis is in no way different from that dictated by the naturalistic hypothesis, then religious faith is a pure superfluity, better pruned away, and controversy about its legitimacy is a piece of idle trifling, unworthy of serious minds. I myself believe, of course, that the religious hypothesis gives to the world an expression which specifically determines our reactions, and makes them in a large part unlike what they might be on a purely naturalistic scheme of belief.

in not trusting to it exclusively, in not waiting for its releasing word. But if we are empiricists, if we believe that no bell in us tolls to let us know for certain when truth is in our grasp, then it seems a piece of idle fantasticality to preach so solemnly our duty of waiting for the bell. Indeed we *may* wait if we will, — I hope you do not think that I am denying that, — but if we do so, we do so at our peril as much as if we believed. In either case we *act*, taking our life in our hands. No one of us ought to issue vetoes to the other, nor should we bandy words of abuse. We ought, on the contrary, delicately and profoundly to respect one another's mental freedom: then only shall we bring about the intellectual republic; then only shall we have that spirit of inner tolerance without which all our outer tolerance is soulless, and which is empiricism's glory; then only shall we live and let live, in speculative as well as in practical things.

I began by a reference to Fitz James Stephen; let me end by a quotation from him. "What do you think of yourself? What do you think of the world? . . . These are questions with which all must deal as it seems good to them. They are riddles of the Sphinx, and in some way or other we must deal with them. . . . In all important transactions of life we have to take a leap in the dark. . . . If we decide to leave the riddles unanswered, that is a choice; if we waver in our answer, that, too, is a choice: but whatever choice we make, we make it at our peril. If a man chooses to turn his back altogether on God and the future, no one can prevent him; no one can show beyond reasonable doubt that he is mistaken. If a man thinks otherwise and acts as he thinks, I do not see that any one can prove that *he* is mistaken. Each must act as he thinks best; and if he is wrong, so much the worse for him. We stand on a mountain pass in the midst of whirling snow and blinding mist, through which we get glimpses now and then of paths which may be deceptive. If we stand still we shall be frozen to death. If we take the wrong road we shall be dashed to pieces. We do not certainly know whether there is any right one. What must we do? 'Be strong and of a good courage.' Act for the best, hope for the best, and take what comes. . . . If death ends all, we cannot meet death better."[1]

[1] Liberty, Equality, Fraternity, p. 353, 2d edition. London, 1874.

An Examination of 'The Will to Believe'

2001

A.J. Burger

"A wise man ... proportions his belief to the evidence."
David Hume, *An Enquiry Concerning Human Understanding*, Section X, Part I.

Part I

The popularity of "The Will to Believe" by William James[1] is not surprising, given the inadequacy of the traditional arguments for the existence of a god or gods, and the strong desire that many people have to believe. James' response is simple and direct: Believe, if one wishes, by *faith*—that is, without evidence. To be sure, he puts restrictions on when he believes that faith is appropriate, but, as shall be seen, his restrictions are by no means adequate to protect others from the pernicious effects of having beliefs in the absence of evidence—that is, having faith.

---

[1] In *The Will to Believe and other essays in popular philosophy*, Longmans, Green & Co., 1897.

To avoid accusations of misrepresentation, it will be well to consider the matter in James' words:

> Let us give the name of *hypothesis* to anything that may be proposed to our belief; and just as the electricians speak of live and dead wires, let us speak of any hypothesis as either *live* or *dead*. A live hypothesis is one which appeals as a real possibility to him to whom it is proposed. If I ask you to believe in the Mahdi, the notion makes no electric connection with your nature, — it refuses to scintillate with any credibility at all. As an hypothesis it is completely dead. To an Arab, however (even if he be not one of the Mahdi's followers), the hypothesis is among the mind's possibilities: it is alive. This shows that deadness and liveness in an hypothesis are not intrinsic properties, but relations to the individual thinker. They are measured by his willingness to act. The maximum of liveness in an hypothesis means willingness to act irrevocably. Practically, that means belief; but there is some believing tendency wherever there is willingness to act at all.
>
> Next, let us call the decision between two hypotheses an *option*. Options may be of several kinds. They may be — 1, *living* or *dead*; 2, *forced* or *avoidable*; 3, *momentous* or *trivial*; and for our purposes we may call an option a *genuine* option when it is of the forced, living, and momentous kind.
>
> 1. A living option is one in which both hypotheses are live ones. If I say to you: "Be a theosophist or be a Mohammedan," it is probably a dead option, because for you neither hypothesis is

likely to be alive. But if I say: "Be an agnostic or be a Christian," it is otherwise: trained as you are, each hypothesis makes some appeal, however small, to your belief.

2. Next, if I say to you: "Choose between going out with your umbrella or without it," I do not offer you a genuine option, for it is not forced. You can easily avoid it by not going out at all. Similarly, if I say, "Either love me or hate me," "Either call my theory true or call it false," your option is avoidable. You may remain indifferent to me, neither loving nor hating, and you may decline to offer any judgment as to my theory. But if I say, "Either accept this truth or go without it," I put on you a forced option, for there is no standing place outside of the alternative. Every dilemma based on a complete logical disjunction, with no possibility of not choosing, is an option of this forced kind.

3. Finally, if I were Dr. Nansen and proposed to you to join my North Pole expedition, your option would be momentous; for this would probably be your only similar opportunity, and your choice now would either exclude you from the North Pole sort of immortality altogether or put at least the chance of it into your hands. He who refuses to embrace a unique opportunity loses the prize as surely as if he tried and failed. *Per contra*, the option is trivial when the opportunity is not unique, when the stake is insignificant, or when the decision is reversible if it later prove unwise. Such trivial options abound in the scientific life. A chemist finds an hypothesis live enough to spend a year in its verification: he believes in it to that extent. But if his experiments prove inconclusive

either way, he is quit for his loss of time, no vital harm being done.

It will facilitate our discussion if we keep all these distinctions well in mind.

...

The thesis I defend is, briefly stated, this: *Our passional nature not only lawfully may, but must, decide an option between propositions, whenever it is a genuine option that cannot by its nature be decided on intellectual grounds; for to say, under such circumstances, "Do not decide, but leave the question open," is itself a passional decision, – just like deciding yes or no, – and is attended with the same risk of losing the truth.* [2-4, 11; 42-44, 51 in this edition]

First, it may be observed that James confuses actions and beliefs. According to James, *hypotheses* are potential beliefs, not actions—potential or otherwise ("Let us give the name of *hypothesis* to anything that may be proposed to our belief..."). An *option* is "the decision between two hypotheses"—that is, a decision between two potential beliefs—not a decision between two potential actions. However, his examples to explain the difference between a *forced option* and an *avoidable option* leave something to be desired, for several involve actions, not beliefs. "'Choose between going out with your umbrella or without it'" is a choice between potential actions, not potential beliefs. The same may be said of his examples to explain the difference between a *momentous option* and a *trivial option*.

The distinction between beliefs and actions is important, so it would be good to consider the matter carefully. If one has the belief that it will rain, one might carry an umbrella because of that belief. We might know about one's beliefs by one's actions, but one's beliefs are distinct from one's actions. For example, if one is carrying an umbrella, this, by itself, is insufficient to warrant the claim that that person believes that it will rain. This person may have just purchased it for future use, or may be returning it to its owner, from whom it was borrowed when it was raining, or any of many other possibilities. Likewise, given the belief that it will rain, one might not carry an umbrella; one might, for example, prefer to use a raincoat and rain hat, or one might have left one's umbrella at the office, or one might not even own an umbrella. All of this is *not* to deny James' claim that one can measure one's belief by one's actions; indeed, how else could one? Also, if beliefs did not affect actions, it would seem to be wholly insignificant what anyone believed. However, it is clear that they do affect actions. Suppose, for example, that you take your car to a mechanic. Would you do this if you did not believe that your car needed a repair, or some maintenance, or simply wanted to be sure that it did not need a repair before going on a trip? (There are, of course, fanciful possibilities, such as being told at gunpoint that you must take your car to a mechanic or else, so that you believe that you might be killed if you do not, etc. But even in this case, there is a belief at the root, so to speak, of the action.) Indeed, one expects to find a belief, or set of beliefs, along with emotions, as the source of the actions of individuals. If a friend were to ask you why you took your car to a mechanic, your friend would naturally expect a belief or set of beliefs as the answer. Were you to say, "For no reason," your friend would be apt not to believe you.

It is also worth mentioning that one who waits for evidence before obtaining a belief might not wait to act. For example, if you are crossing a road, and a car is racing toward you, you may need to act quickly—either continue across or return to the side from which you came—but you do *not* need to *believe* that you have made the correct choice in order to act. One may need to act without much evidence, but one need not believe with insufficient evidence. All one need believe, in this case, is that if one wishes to live, it will be most effective to get out of the path of the speeding car—a fact for which one has abundant evidence. One may act without first believing that the choice will turn out for the best. This will generally be true in cases where one has evidence that one needs to act quickly, but lacks evidence about what action would be best. Consequently, emergencies do not require faith, but rather actions based upon the best available evidence. Of course, in such cases, one may make the wrong choice and be run over by the car—but, then, *believing* that one would not be run over would not help.

It is to be hoped that the remarks above will suffice to clarify the distinction between beliefs and actions.

Second, there are probably good reasons for doubting whether the options that James had in mind when referring to an "*option that cannot by its nature be decided on intellectual grounds*" [11; *51 in this edition*] really cannot be decided on intellectual grounds. For example, the Problem of Evil is surely relevant to the belief in an omniscient, omnipotent, perfectly benevolent god. How could there be such a god, given the fact that there is evil? If there were such a god, it would know about the evil, being omniscient; it would have the power to prevent the evil, being omnipotent; and it would have the inclination to prevent the evil, being perfectly benevolent; consequently, there would be no evil if there were such a god, because such a god would prevent all evil; as there is evil, this proves that there is no omniscient, omnipotent, perfectly benevolent god. (For a more complete discussion of this, see *Dialogues Concerning Natural Religion* by David Hume, especially Parts X and XI; *Superstition in All Ages* by Jean Meslier, AKA Baron d'Holbach; *The Atheist Debater's Handbook* by B.C. Johnson, particularly section XII; or even *Candide* by Voltaire or *The Brothers Karamozov* by Fyodor Dostoevsky.) This issue will not be pursued here, as it is 'controversial' and unnecessary for the present purposes.

James' remarks (omitted in the quote above) about many beliefs not being an act of will or volition seem quite correct—along with his remarks about the influence of sentiments in some cases [see sections II & III, p. 4-11; *p. 44-50 in this edition*]. (Incidentally, these sections are often not reprinted in anthologies containing most of James' essay.)

James' statements about the distinction between knowing the truth and avoiding error are another matter:

> There are two ways of looking at our duty in the matter of opinion, − ways entirely different, and yet ways about whose difference the theory of knowledge seems hitherto to have shown very little concern. *We must know the truth;* and *we must avoid error,* − these are our first and great commandments as would-be knowers; but they are not two ways of stating an identical commandment, they are two separable laws. Although it may indeed happen that when we believe the truth *A*, we escape as an incidental consequence from believing the falsehood *B*, it hardly ever happens that by merely disbelieving *B* we necessarily believe *A*. We may in escaping *B* fall into believing other

falsehoods, C or D, just as bad as B; or we may escape B by not believing anything at all, not even A.

... Believe nothing, he [Clifford] tells us, keep your mind in suspense forever, rather than by closing it on insufficient evidence incur the awful risk of believing lies. You, on the other hand, may think that the risk of being in error is a very small matter when compared with the blessings of real knowledge, and be ready to be duped many times in your investigation rather than postpone indefinitely the chance of guessing true. I myself find it impossible to go with Clifford. [17-18; *56-57 in this edition*]

There are two comments we may make about this. First, James is quite confused about what "real knowledge" is. It is *not* merely guessing correctly, but necessarily involves reason and evidence. Imagine, for example, there were six people, who, by faith, each formed a different belief about the outcome of a single fair roll of a fair die, so that each person believed that the outcome would be a different number. Excluding the possibility of the die not landing flat, we can be certain that five of the six would be wrong and one would be correct regarding the outcome. However, all of them, before the event, were equally unjustified in their belief. A person who had real knowledge of such a situation would believe that each of the six possible outcomes would be equally likely. To believe otherwise is to show a lack of understanding and knowledge of the situation. Curiously, James apparently believed that a belief based on a random guess, but that turns out to be true, is an example of "real knowledge," despite the fact that such a belief really demonstrates ignorance or extreme foolishness. (One may, of course, bet on an outcome without believing in advance that that outcome will necessarily occur; this should always be kept in mind, for although beliefs affect actions, beliefs are different from actions.) The person with the true belief in the outcome of the die roll, far from having real knowledge, is really demonstrating the opposite. The person with real knowledge in this situation, and many others of a like nature, necessarily suspends judgment—which is something James seems loathe to do, despite it being often the most sensible course. James instead preferred to commit the logical fallacy of argumentum ad ignorantium (also known as "appeal to ignorance"); because it had not been proven to James' satisfaction that certain propositions that he wished to believe are false, he concluded that they are true (as believing a statement is regarding that statement as true). Because he does not know the answer to questions that are important to him, he makes a bigoted guess and calls it "real knowledge" if his guess turns out to be true.

The second comment we may make about this is that the two "commandments," "*We must know the truth;* and *we must avoid error*," are *not* "entirely different," as James imagines, but are only very slightly different. If one is to find the truth about any matter, one must avoid error. If one is in error about anything, one necessarily has lost the truth about it. Now, it is true that one may avoid error and still not gain the truth, but this only occurs when one suspends judgment about the matter. If one does not suspend judgment, then finding the truth and avoiding error are in fact identical. Apparently James did not like to suspend judgment; he would rather make a bigoted and prejudiced guess than be intellectually honest and admit to himself that he does not really know. Imagine a bigot, who hated all black people, believing because of his bigotry that a particular black person was a thief and a scoundrel. It may turn out, in a particular case, to happen to be true that that individual was a thief and a scoundrel (as there are thieves and scoundrels of every color), but that would in no way justify the belief that was based upon prejudice and bigotry. Yet, according to James, this bigotry is an example of "real knowledge," as he evidently considers "guessing true" to be "real knowledge," even though such guessing often results in false beliefs, which even James admits ("... be ready to be duped many times...").

In view of this, we see that James' later remark about the seriousness of error is quite mistaken: "Our errors are surely not such awfully solemn things." [19; *58 in this edition*] Obviously, they are, given the actions that often result from such prejudiced beliefs, such as those of the Inquisition, which even James mentioned earlier [17; *56 in this edition*], though he obviously failed to appreciate the significance of his own example.

James' remarks about having 'scientific' beliefs only when one has evidential support seem quite unobjectionable. However, he does seem to be mistaken about the best attitude of a scientist for accurate discoveries. He states:

> On the other hand, if you want an absolute duffer in an investigation, you must, after all, take the man who has no interest whatever in its results: he is the warranted incapable, the positive fool. The most useful investigator, because the most sensitive observer, is always he whose eager interest in one side of the question is balanced by an equally keen nervousness lest he become deceived. [21; *60 in this edition*]

Would it not be better if the scientist simply wishes to find out, with no interest in which outcome occurs? The scientist who is curious to simply find out is far superior to the scientist who has an interest in one side of an issue, no matter how "nervous" he or she is about being deceived, for that interest interferes with objectivity. James is right in stating that one who does not care about the results will not be apt to be very competent (if, in fact, this is what he means), but James is giving a false dilemma, or bifurcation, when he omits the possibility of a scientist who is interested in the results out of curiosity, but does not care what way the experiment turns out.

No doubt James is correct in affirming that there are truths that one will never believe if one only has beliefs based upon evidence. For example, you, the reader, will probably never believe the truth about what beverage I am consuming as I write this sentence. But what does it matter? Even if it is a matter of importance to you, such as whether your spouse (if you have one) is cheating on you or not, would it be wise to jump to some conclusion prior to obtaining any evidence regarding the matter? Would it not be best to be especially careful regarding important matters? Yet James recommends the exact opposite, for he advocates faith regarding momentous options. Obviously, this is not an example of something that cannot be decided on intellectual grounds; the point is simply that one ought to be most careful about what is most important, not the reverse, as James imagines.

Consider James' remarks in the following:

> Turn now from these wide questions of good to a certain class of questions of fact, questions concerning personal relations, states of mind

between one man and another. *Do you like me or not?* — for example. Whether you do or not depends, in countless instances, on whether I meet you half-way, am willing to assume that you must like me, and show you trust and expectation. The previous faith on my part in your liking's existence is in such cases what makes your liking come. But if I stand aloof, and refuse to budge an inch until I have objective evidence, until you shall have done something apt, as the absolutists say, *ad extorquendum assensum meum*, ten to one your liking never comes. How many women's hearts are vanquished by the mere sanguine insistence of some man that they *must* love him! he will not consent to the hypothesis that they cannot. The desire for a certain kind of truth here brings about that special truth's existence; and so it is in innumerable cases of other sorts. Who gains promotions, boons, appointments, but the man in whose life they are seen to play the part of live hypotheses, who discounts them, sacrifices other things for their sake before they have come, and takes risks for them in advance? His faith acts on the powers above him as a claim, and creates its own verification.

A social organism of any sort whatever, large or small, is what it is because each member proceeds to his own duty with a trust that the other members will simultaneously do theirs. Wherever a desired result is achieved by the co-operation of many independent persons, its existence as a fact is a pure consequence of the precursive faith in one another of those immediately concerned. A government, an army, a commercial system, a ship, a college, an athletic team, all exist on this condition, without which not only is nothing achieved, but nothing is even attempted.   A whole train of passengers (individually brave enough) will be looted by a few highwaymen, simply because the latter can count on one another, while each passenger fears that if he makes a movement of resistance, he will be shot before any one else backs him up.   If we believed that the whole car-full would rise at once with us, we should each severally rise, and train-robbing would never even be attempted.   There are, then, cases where a fact cannot come at all unless a preliminary faith exists in its coming.   *And where faith in a fact can help create the fact,* that would be an insane logic which should say that faith running ahead of scientific evidence is the 'lowest kind of immorality' into which a thinking being can fall. Yet such is the logic by which our scientific absolutists pretend to regulate our lives!

X.

In truths dependent on our personal action, then, faith based on desire is certainly a lawful and possibly an indispensable thing.   [23-25; *62-64 in this edition*]

First, it may be observed, that these examples where, supposedly, "*faith in a fact can help create the fact,*" do not fit in with the thesis that James is supposedly defending, for they are not by their nature such that they cannot be decided on intellectual grounds.   "*Do you like me or not?*" is a question which, generally, can be decided on intellectual grounds. Thus it lies outside the realm of those beliefs that are covered by his own thesis. Evidently, then, James is contradicting himself by these affirmations, as he apparently forbade such beliefs earlier in his essay when he stated his thesis. I say "apparently," as James' thesis merely states when one may have faith, not when one may not; though it may be presumed that he intended that one may not have faith in other cases not covered in his thesis; otherwise, why not include those other legitimate cases of faith in his thesis? It would have been good if he had stated his exact position clearly, but it is hardly surprising that he did not, given his carelessness about so many matters in his essay.

But there is more wrong with these examples, which leads to a second criticism. James again is guilty of bifurcation, or false dilemma, when he represents the only possibilities being either having the belief that you like me or I stand aloof. Granted, if I stand aloof, you may never come to like me, but I can be friendly without assuming that you like me. And, if I trust people without any evidence that they are trustworthy, they are rather likely to take advantage of me or hold me in contempt for being such a ridiculous fool and, to borrow a phrase from James, 'ten to one their liking never comes.' After all, who wishes to have a fool for a friend? Again, this problem seems to be the result of James' confusion regarding beliefs and actions, for one can believe that you are not a friend, but act like you are or could become one. The important beliefs to have in such a situation include: 1) You may come to like me, particularly if I behave in a likable way; or you may not; and 2) You may turn out to be untrustworthy, so I ought not trust you too much with anything I value highly; or you may turn out to be trustworthy. Not having the belief that you like me does not entail having the belief that you do not like me; one may have no belief about it at all, or, in other words, be an agnostic with respect to that question.

Third, consider:

> Who gains promotions, boons, appointments, but the man in whose life they are seen to play the part of *live hypotheses* [italics added], who discounts them, sacrifices other things for their sake before they have come, and takes risks for them in advance? His *faith* [italics added] acts on the powers above him as a claim, and creates its own verification. [24; *63 in this edition*]

As James earlier defined the term, "A live hypothesis is one which appeals as a real possibility to him to whom it is proposed." [2; *42 in this edition*] The belief that something is a *possibility* is far different from having faith that it is or will be so. One may agree with what is suggested by the first of these sentences and reject the second. Indeed, if one already believes that it is or necessarily will be so, why would one sacrifice other things or take risks to bring about what one already has or necessarily will have? Clearly, one would not, which brings us to what really "acts on the powers above him as a claim," which are the *actions* of sacrificing other things and taking risks to bring them about. It is actions that get things done (for which there is abundant evidence), and one who believes this will be apt to act to get what one desires. No faith is necessary or useful here; indeed, faith positively gets in the way, as mentioned above, for such faith may impede action. Thus, faith in a fact does not help create the fact; it is actions that create the fact.

Fourth, when a "social organism" works through cooperation, with each member trusting that at least some of the others will do their part, one often has such a belief not as faith, but based upon evidence which one has gathered from one's interactions with others. From one's earliest youth, one has observed that people often do cooperate, and one may have an idea of when and in what ways and under what circumstances people commonly cooperate with each other. When one observes an athletic team (to use one of James' examples), one naturally expects a certain form of cooperation. Such a belief is based upon evidence, not on faith (or nothing).

Fifth, if all of a sudden, all of the passengers on a train, who are being threatened by highwaymen, rose up in resistance, very probably a number of the passengers would be killed rather than simply robbed. (Incidentally, the train robbers can loot the whole train not "simply because . . . [they] can count on one another" and the passengers cannot, but because the robbers are armed and the passengers are not.) Would such a result, the outcome of what James apparently regards as a noble faith, be better than the loss of a few possessions? Eventually, perhaps, train robbing would no longer even be attempted if all passengers behaved in such a manner. However, believing that everyone would rise up together would be believing not only without evidence, but against the evidence. Other examples of belief against the evidence, this 'mad-dog' faith, include believing that one's head is made of wood, that a human can fly without the aid of any devices, and any other absurdities that the most fanciful imagination can devise. If you were on a train that was being robbed and you had the mad-dog faith that James admires, you would very probably be shot by the highwaymen.

Thus it may be said that faith is not indispensable, contrary to what James seems to suggest.

But all these matters, so far, are not what seems to have motivated James to write his essay, nor is it the end of his folly. Consider:

> But now, it will be said, these are all childish human cases, and have nothing to do with great cosmical matters, like the question of religious faith. Let us then pass on to that. Religions differ so much in their accidents that in discussing the religious question we must make it very generic and broad. What then do we now mean by the religious hypothesis? Science says things are; morality says some things are better than other things; and religion says essentially two things.
>
> First, she says that the best things are the more eternal things, the overlapping things, the things in the universe that throw the last stone, so to speak, and say the final word. "Perfection is eternal," — this phrase of Charles Secrétan seems a good way of putting this first affirmation of religion, an affirmation which obviously cannot yet be verified scientifically at all.
>
> The second affirmation of religion is that we are better off even now if we believe her first affirmation to be true. [25-26; *64 in this edition*]

The first "thing" religion says, to wit, "the best things are the more eternal things," is demonstrably false. All one need consider is the relative value of eternal pain and a momentary pleasure to know that duration, by itself, is wholly irrelevant to whether something is better or worse. (In general, at least, it may be said that good things are better when, all else being equal, they last longer, but bad things are worse when, all else being equal, they last longer.) Undoubtedly, someone will wish to defend James by giving his remarks some mystical meaning—which is to say, no meaning at all. The second affirmation of religion, which can be seen to state that we are better off if we believe something that is demonstrably false (the first affirmation of religion), now seems wholly improbable. Were we to really believe it, we might prefer nuclear waste to wholesome, ripe fruit.

James' remarks about the benefits of religion—which is really a good deal more robust than one might think from his remarks above about the "religious hypothesis"—need not be examined here. The disadvantages of religion have been laboriously enumerated elsewhere—the opposition to freedom, the opposition to science and advances in knowledge, the torture, oppression, and murder of innocents by various religious groups including the Holy Office of the Roman Catholic Church (more commonly called the Inquisition, which was started in the 13th century under Pope Innocent III, and whose governing body, the Congregation of the Holy Office, still exists to this day[1]—

---

[1]   The remarks in the text are taken from *The Oxford English Dictionary*, 1971, *Compact Edition*, Vol. 1, p. 1444 (in the non-compact version, Vol. I-K, p. 324). The Roman Catholic Church has, however, renamed the Congregation of the Holy Office, now calling it the Congregation for the Doctrine of the Faith. This has led many people to the erroneous belief that this institution has been abolished. (This is not the first time that its name has been changed, which makes research into its origin and history much more difficult, which undoubtedly is desired by the Catholic Church, as keeping the truth about such things in greater obscurity may save some embarrassment.) Its lists of banned literature are not made easily available to the public, evidently to avoid

so it cannot reasonably be called a momentary aberration of religion—and whose function is still the same—to suppress heresy, though its methods have been curtailed with the loss of influence of the Church), etc.

One must take care when reading James in order to avoid being misled about his position from carelessly chosen expressions. For example:

> But sad experience makes me fear that some of you may still shrink from radically saying with me, *in abstracto,* that we have the right to believe at our own risk any hypothesis that is live enough to tempt our will. [29; *67 in this edition*]

If this were the position that James were defending—that we may have faith whenever we wish—it would not have been necessary for him to introduce his distinctions regarding a "genuine option." This particular quote also shows the self-centeredness of James—no concern is expressed for how the belief might affect others. We may believe "at our own risk"—but what about the risk to others?

Still, some might be seduced by James' noble-sounding words:

> No one of us ought to issue vetoes to the other, *nor should we bandy words of abuse* [italics added]. We ought, on the contrary, delicately and profoundly to respect one another's mental freedom: then only

---

the just ridicule of such practices. Much of its activity is hidden and shrouded in mystery, though it clearly pressures individuals within the Church to comply with its demands.

shall we bring about the intellectual republic; then only shall we have that spirit of inner tolerance without which all our outer tolerance is soulless, and which is empiricism's glory; then only shall we live and let live, in speculative as well as in practical things. [30; *69 in this edition*]

James seems to have forgotten some of his own remarks contained earlier in his essay, such as:

> *And where faith in a fact can help create the fact,* that would be an *insane* [italics added] logic which should say that faith running ahead of scientific evidence is the 'lowest kind of immorality' into which a thinking being can fall. *Yet such is the logic by which our scientific absolutists pretend to regulate our lives* [italics added]! [25; *64 in this edition*]

And:

> If the [religious] hypothesis *were* true in all its parts, including this one, then pure intellectualism, with its veto on our making willing advances, would be an absurdity; and some participation of our sympathetic nature would be logically required. I, therefore, for one, cannot see my way to accepting the agnostic rules for truth-seeking, or wilfully agree to keep my willing nature out of the game. I cannot do so for this plain reason, that *a rule of thinking which would absolutely prevent me from acknowledging certain kinds of truth if those kinds of truth were really there, would be an irrational rule.* [28; *67 in this edition*]

If calling "scientific absolutists" and "pure intellectualism" "insane," "an absurdity," and "irrational" is not to "bandy words of abuse," then nothing is.

James' hypocrisy should, however, come as no surprise, for although he claims to be writing in favor of tolerance, he is in reality defending bigotry—bigotry is "obstinate or *blind* [italics added] attachment to a particular creed."[1]   In other words, faith is bigotry, and it should come as no surprise that such an advocate would have many hateful and damning beliefs.

Part II

Now it might well be said that, whatever flaws there are in James' examples and other parts of his essay, it does not prove that his basic thesis is incorrect. *Proofs* in ethics are hard to come by, and one ought not expect to find this essay different from others in this respect.   However, the consequences of his thesis may be very easily examined, and they are such that few, if any, would be willing to accept.

Consider:

> The thesis I defend is, briefly stated, this: *Our passional nature not only lawfully may, but must, decide*

---

[1] *Webster's New Universal Unabridged Dictionary*, 2nd edition, Dorset & Baber, p. 181.

> *an option between propositions, whenever it is a genuine*
> *option that cannot by its nature be decided on*
> *intellectual grounds; for to say, under such*
> *circumstances, "Do not decide, but leave the question*
> *open," is itself a passional decision, – just like deciding*
> *yes or no, – and is attended with the same risk of losing*
> *the truth.* [11; *51 in this edition*]

The restrictions on when it is appropriate to believe in something without evidence, or have faith, are put there by James in order to protect others from beliefs with pernicious consequences, that is, from beliefs that lead to pernicious actions.[1] But are his restrictions sufficient?

The following real-life example is from an Associated Press story of a few years ago. In Auburn, Maine, a woman and her live-in boyfriend were charged with murdering the woman's four-year-old daughter by burning her alive in their oven. According to neighbors, there were loud religious music, sounds of fighting, banging, and screams of "Let me out!" and "Let me out, Daddy, let me out!" emanating from their apartment. One neighbor reported being told by the boyfriend that "Lucifer" was burning in the oven when she asked about the smell coming from the apartment. According to police, when they arrived, smoke and the odor of burned human flesh filled the apartment, and the child was dead.

---

[1] See "The Ethics of Belief" by William Kingdon Clifford, and "The Will to Believe" by William James, which was written as a response to ideas like those in Clifford's essay, in which Clifford describes a ship owner who has *faith* that his ship is safe, so he sends it out to sea without inspecting it, with predictable results.

From these facts, the probable events may be reconstructed.[1] The couple apparently believed that the four-year-old was the devil named "Lucifer" and that Lucifer could be killed by being burned in their oven. They also believed that, as Lucifer is evil and responsible for all, or most, or a substantial amount of the bad things that occur in the world, and would get away and cause more evil if they did not kill him immediately, they would be doing the world a favor by killing him—and a disservice if they let him get away. (Notice how the killing of Lucifer follows quite reasonably from these beliefs.) We may now ask, according to James' thesis, did they have the right to have the beliefs that led them to kill the four-year-old girl?

First, was it, for them, a living option to have the belief or to refrain from having the belief that the girl was Lucifer (along with the accompanying beliefs)? James defined an hypothesis as:

> anything that may be proposed to our belief …. A live hypothesis is one which appeals as a real possibility to him to whom it is proposed. … deadness and liveness in an hypothesis are not intrinsic properties, but relations to the individual thinker. [2-3; *42 in this edition*]

As they apparently really did believe that the girl was Lucifer, that must have been, for them, a living hypothesis, as it appealed to them as a real possibility; and as, presumably, it was a living hypothesis for them to not believe she was Lucifer, it was, for them, a living option.

[1] And if this "reconstruction" is not what really happened, it *could* have happened this way, which is all that is required for the present purposes.

Second, was it a forced option? Well, they either
believe that she is Lucifer or they do not believe that she
is Lucifer, so it is a forced option. (Notice how any
hypothesis, teamed with the negation of believing that
hypothesis, form a forced option.)[1]

Third, was it a momentous option? Well, the
opportunity was unique, for, among other things, Lucifer
could escape if they did not act immediately. The stakes
were significant, for it surely matters whether a four-year-
old girl or Lucifer is killed by being burned alive.
Furthermore, the decision was irreversible if it should later
prove unwise. As these three qualities are what James
requires for an option to be momentous, it was a
momentous option.

And as a genuine option is one that is living, forced, and
momentous, it was a genuine option.

We are not yet at the point where we may justly affirm
that by James' thesis they were justified in their belief that
the child was Lucifer. For it is not any genuine option that
is allowed by his thesis; it is only a genuine option *"that
cannot by its nature be decided on intellectual grounds."*

---

[1] If it be objected that not believing something is not a belief, and,
therefore, the choice between having a belief or not having that belief
will not be an option, the reply is simple: Although that is, strictly
speaking, correct, it must be ignored if we are to proceed at all. *For,
otherwise, nothing could possibly be a forced option.* No matter what
two particular potential beliefs are presented as an option, one can
always reject both, and simply have no belief about the matter at all.
Consequently, on this strict interpretation of James' thesis, *no* instance
of faith is permitted, for only hypotheses that are part of *genuine
options*—which are always *forced options*—are we permitted to believe
without evidence. Indeed, James' example of a forced option is exactly
like the one here in this respect.

Well, can the question of whether the child was Lucifer or not be decided on intellectual grounds? What test could be given? If the child behaves abnormally, it could be Lucifer or it could simply be an abnormal child. If the child behaves normally, it could be a normal child, or it could be Lucifer pretending to be a child as a disguise. No matter what the child does, then—or what it looks like—one cannot tell whether it is Lucifer or not. Thus it is a question that cannot by its nature be decided on intellectual grounds. And as it was a genuine option, then, according to James' thesis, they were justified in their beliefs. And as their actions follow naturally and reasonably from their beliefs, it would be ridiculous to condemn the one without condemning the other, so it may be said that, according to James' thesis, they were fully justified in what they did.

And, indeed, everyone who encourages faith may be said to be partly responsible for the actions of this couple, and others like them. For to encourage faith is to encourage such beliefs, which lead inevitably to such actions. It will in vain be objected that they were not encouraged to believe *what* they believed, for they were encouraged to believe *how* they believed. And once faith is believed to be acceptable, there can be no justifiable restrictions on what is to be believed, for to ask, 'Why have faith in this rather than that?' is to ask for reasons or evidence for the belief—which is to give up on having faith. And, indeed, the couple who burned alive the four-year-old girl had as much reason for their beliefs as many others who imagine themselves innocent—or even virtuous—for having faith.

It will be no use to object that they were "insane," for, first, why would one suppose that? Is it because they did not have evidence for their beliefs—because they had faith? Besides, this is in reality the same kind of belief as the doctrine of transubstantiation—the official doctrine of the Roman Catholic Church, where the bread and wine of the Eucharist ceremony are said to be literally changed into the body and blood of Jesus while maintaining all of the physical properties, including the appearance, of bread and wine. And second, James' thesis justifies such beliefs, regardless of whether or not one would necessarily be "insane" to have such beliefs.

It will also be of no use to object that to say that one who believes something for which no evidence could possibly be obtained, either for or against, is to say that one believes nonsense, for that would mean that James' thesis only justifies belief in nonsense.

One might claim that James would object to what these people believed. However that may be, it has no bearing on the question of whether the position that he stated would support such beliefs. Indeed, such an objection would amount to stating that James, had he understood its implications, would reject his own thesis.

It might also be objected that it would be acceptable to follow James' thesis as long as no one would get hurt. First, that is not the position that James states; it is a different one. And secondly, and more importantly, how could one tell if someone got hurt? After all, if the couple had burned Lucifer, then they did not harm a little girl at all. The belief that they did harm to a little girl comes only from rejecting their faith that it was Lucifer. Thus, not only is the rejection of faith necessary for preventing harm, but the rejection of faith is necessary for even noticing the harm that is done. Therefore, if we are to avoid harming others, we must reject faith.

Now, as, according to James' thesis, the couple was fully justified in their beliefs, and by implication, in the actions that follow naturally and rationally from those beliefs, it may be concluded that either they were justified or James is wrong. And as most people would emphatically deny that they were justified, then it can be said that, according to most people, at least, James is wrong. Indeed, when one considers its implications, no one but a monster could find James' thesis acceptable.

Our beliefs affect our actions, and our actions affect others. As we are responsible for our actions, we are responsible for the beliefs that prompt our actions. Our beliefs also affect what beliefs we might have in the future. No one can fairly investigate a question who has a belief about it not based upon evidence—or even, as Clifford says, who wishes to believe one side of a question. Also, by having faith about some matters, we set up a habit of having faith and being indifferent to evidence. We do not have beliefs in isolation; one belief affects our other beliefs; it makes us prone to accept others of a like nature, and reject beliefs dissimilar to it, and so one belief affects all our beliefs, like a small pebble producing ripples in a pond, affecting its whole surface. By setting a bad example to others, we encourage them to like errors, so that, even if it were possible to act on one's faith no more than by a statement here and there, the effects upon society will be incalculable. Because of the possible effects of our beliefs upon society, it is our duty to believe only in proportion to the evidence. We have no right to be so careless and irresponsible regarding matters that affect society so profoundly.

Having beliefs, rather than doubts, is more comfortable and agreeable to most people, which explains why many are apt to acquire beliefs that soothe, rather than remain in doubt until evidence about the matter can be obtained—if, indeed, any evidence can be obtained.

To encourage beliefs without evidence is to sow the seeds of the destruction of society. Experiments in irrationality have occurred countless times in history, leading to death and destruction, but as technology progresses, the potential devastating effects become far greater. One memorable example from the 20th century involves the Nazis in Germany. One was to believe in the Party regardless of the evidence—and, indeed, many did not believe the enormities of the crimes in concentration camps and elsewhere—despite having evidence of what was happening. And one who does not believe that something is happening will surely do nothing to stop it.

Nothing can justify a belief that is not based upon evidence: It is a sin against humanity. To lose the ability to test things and to question everything is to sink into savagery. No one can love truth and be so careless about it as to believe anything without evidence. A concern for the truth gives an interest in evidence, lest one should lose that which one loves, and let one's belief fall upon some unworthy object. "What is wanted is not the will to believe, but the will to find out, which is the exact opposite."[1] Every action, every sentence, every word, every belief, may serve for the preservation of society—or rend it in pieces.

It is immoral to have faith—to prejudge matters before one has evidence. Faith is prejudice—"a judgment or opinion formed before the facts are known."[2]

[1] Bertrand Russell, "Free Thought and Official Propaganda", in *Skeptical Essays*, 1928, W.W. Norton & Co., Inc., p. 157.
[2] *Webster's New Universal Unabridged Dictionary*, 2nd edition, Dorset & Baber, p. 1420.

Lest anyone object that the example of the child being burned alive in the oven is too "exotic," and therefore somehow lacking in validity regarding this matter of faith, consider an example already mentioned in passing: The Inquisition. As the Inquisition, or Holy Office, lasted, in its full splendor and glory, for several hundred years, it cannot be justly regarded as too "exotic" or an aberration. Given the faith that one has an immortal soul that will suffer eternal torment if one does not believe, and the relative unimportance of this life when compared with eternity, it follows that doing anything to get people to believe is doing them a favor. Thus, if torture will get them to believe, then torturing them is doing them a favor. Or, if one believes that by torturing "heretics," more people will pretend to believe, which, as no one voices a contrary opinion, will encourage more people to believe, then one may torture to save some souls, even if the ones being tortured cannot be "saved." (Incidentally, such a belief seems plausible from the evidence of history.) And, in any case, such heretics, according to the faithful, deserve to suffer anyway, so that no wrong is done in using them in such a manner. After all, if they did not deserve to suffer, God would not damn them to Hell for eternal punishment. (Notice that the parts of this requiring faith can form a genuine option that cannot by their nature be decided on intellectual grounds, so that this is permitted by James' thesis.) The Inquisitors were simply acting upon their faith—as, indeed, all who have faith act upon it. Their activities follow quite naturally and rationally from such beliefs as had been acquired by faith, and the only way to stop such action is either by changing their beliefs or by taking away their power to act with impunity. The latter of these two, historically, is what happened, and explains why its ruling body, the

Congregation of the Holy Office, has had its activities significantly curtailed, even though its basic objective remains the same—the suppression of heresy—which is now primarily effected, insofar as it is effected, by banning works of literature and art. When I was in graduate school, a fellow student stated, with apparent sincerity, that he believed that the Inquisition was good. And, indeed, the only way to disagree with him is to reject, at least in part, the faith of the Inquisitors. "Men never do evil so completely and cheerfully as when they do it from religious conviction."[1]

No doubt there will be some who will still insist upon the justifiability of beliefs without evidence because of their desire to believe something for which they have no evidence. This, however, will simply show how stubborn and unreasonable they are. Irrational people do not accept the conclusions of rational arguments, and one may expect that their behavior will follow their beliefs.

Part III

It is clear that more needs to be said about why one would require reasons or evidence for beliefs, rather than simply having beliefs without evidence—that is, having faith. The reason for this is not hard to understand—it

---

[1]   Blaise Pascal, *Pensées*, translated by W.F. Trotter, The Modern Library, 1941, section XIV, no. 894, p. 314.

becomes very clear when one is presented with potential beliefs that are in conflict with each other. Should you trust your friend or not? Here we see the utter impossibility of doing both (at the same time, with respect to the same attribute), for one either trusts someone or one does not. And if one trusts someone to a limited extent, then one is trusting that someone—it cannot truthfully be said that one does not trust that person at all. But which should one choose—to trust or not to trust? If one simply chooses, without regard to reason and evidence, why does one choose what one chooses? Why not choose the opposite? Or in matters of religion, if one chooses to be a Muslim, rather than a Christian or some other alternative, by faith, rather than with evidence, why choose those beliefs rather than any others? To see the need for evidence in matters of religion, one need only consider that the various religions all contradict each other, and, therefore, they cannot all be true. And why choose one religion rather than another? When a believer is attempting to convert others, what can be said to someone who claims faith in another religion? The believer can say that only his or her faith is faith in something true, but that is no evidence at all, and the prospective convert can make the same *claim* about his or her own religion. The religionist who advocates faith is, therefore, in a rather interesting position—he or she must also advocate rejecting faith. The reason for this is clear from the above remarks—one must reject all conflicting faiths if one is to embrace a particular faith. This may be obscured by the fact that people are often inconsistent (and consequently they are necessarily wrong no matter what the truth might be), but it does not alter the fact that, for example, it is impossible to fully embrace both Catholicism and Buddhism, or even Catholicism and Lutheranism.

Anyone who is acquainted with the doctrines of each of these religions will be able to come up with examples of how the doctrine of each conflicts with that of the others. And, indeed, all different religions have conflicting doctrines, for, after all, if their doctrines were all the same, then they would not be different religions.

Furthermore, as one considers that the number of *possible* religions is limitless, it becomes clear that if one randomly (or by faith) chooses one possible religion over the others, one is virtually certain to choose a false religion. For all religions that contradict the truth are false religions, so, at most, one religion is true. And if one were to object that one does not need to be exactly correct in one's choice, how close to the truth must one be? And how could one possibly know that one can be somewhat in error? But the answer to these difficulties becomes irrelevant when one considers that, unless total error is acceptable, one is still unlikely to randomly (or by faith) select one religion over the others that is 'true enough,' for they differ greatly in their claims. There is not, for example, universal agreement that there is an afterlife or even a god, much less agreement on the nature of an afterlife or god. Besides, if being correct is not necessary, then one might as well give up on religion entirely and sleep in on Sunday or whatever day one might attend services, and save one's money for other things. It is ridiculous for people to claim that one can be wrong and still maintain that one must be religious, but this only illustrates their inconsistency and irrationality.

Many religionists seem, nevertheless, to advocate faith in their religions due to a perceived lack of evidence for the basic doctrines that they believe and wish to inculcate in others. This is, no doubt, due to the influence of the arguments of people like David Hume and Immanuel

Kant, but it does leave those particular religionists in a rather unenviable position—they are advocating belief in something for which they themselves believe there is no evidence.   This leaves them with no alternative to advocating faith—that is, belief without evidence—unless they resort to dishonesty regarding the evidence, or they reject their own religious beliefs.   Thus they end up being advocates of faith, though they must, as remarked above, advocate rejecting faith in conflicting beliefs.

For those who believe that there is evidence for their religious beliefs, there is no need to appeal to faith, for they can simply point out that which they believe to be evidence for their position.   They will also be motivated to encourage others to look at evidence rather than have faith, for they want others to reject faith in other religions and have no need of it for their own religion.   These people, therefore, will welcome writings such as Clifford's, which argue that beliefs without evidence are immoral, or, in other words, that it is immoral to have faith.   Such a position favors beliefs for which one can have evidence, which is what this sort of religionist believes of his or her religion.

It is worth noting that religionists of a certain type are not the only ones who perceive some benefits of having faith.   Manufacturers of bad products also benefit from people having beliefs without evidence, and must therefore encourage, or at least keep quiet in a culture that favors faith, for the sake of company profits.   After all, if people were to acquire beliefs only after they had evidence for them, then they would not be so apt to buy low-quality products, for they would not believe them to be worth buying until they had evidence in favor of such beliefs.   It is better for such companies that people acquire beliefs from feeling and sentiment, so that they can put out pleasing advertisements and other propaganda that will get people to make unwise purchases. And, clearly, this is applicable to the majority of manufacturers, for whatever product is produced, there is, generally speaking, a wide variety of undesirable choices when one shops. Most cars, for example, fall far short of the reliability of the most reliable car; though it is true that different circumstances will make different choices more desirable. Nevertheless, it may be stated with a very high degree of assurance that most cars are not a good choice for anyone. And this applies to virtually all other products as well. As a consequence of this, most manufacturers benefit from people making unwise choices, for otherwise, they would often not sell anything at all. Naturally, this means that manufacturers of good products are harmed by consumers' faith, but they constitute a relatively small percentage of the total number of manufacturers. And, of course, consumers are also harmed by bad choices; both because they have a lesser quality product, and because they are thereby supporting manufacturers of bad products, which in turn makes future shopping more difficult. The future difficulties in shopping are not hard to understand—by purchasing bad products, the makers of those products are kept in business, and they are motivated to continue manufacturing bad products, because they are selling—which is, after all, the primary objective for most businesses. Thus the future possible choices will include many worthless products as well. If, on the other hand, people made wise choices in the purchase of manufactured (and other) goods, the companies that persisted in making bad products would lose money and eventually go out of business (unless, of course, they also made worthwhile products, but then they would only profit from their good products, so that they would be motivated to make the good and not the bad products). Thus, when shopping in the future, one would not have as great a need to be so very careful in the purchase of new products, because only the manufacturers of worthwhile products will have remained in business. Some care will still be necessary, for it will always be possible that some new product will be of inferior quality, but the market would favor high-quality items. This means that not only are people who make bad choices in their purchases harmed, but even people who make reasoned purchases are harmed by the bad choices of others because of the continued presence in the market of so many bad choices to avoid. It further harms everyone because, instead of attempting to make better products to compete with other manufacturers, companies now are able to sell some worthless gizmo. The result is fewer good products, and even the best of what is currently available would probably be inferior to what would be available if people only made reasoned choices because more companies would probably be competing to make the best possible products.

The same may be said of many U.S. politicians. Many of our elected officials could never reasonably hope to be elected if their constituents formed beliefs about them based solely on evidence. As most voters embrace faith as a mode of belief formation, they inevitably elect people who say what the voters wish to hear, yet do what is not in the public interest. The politicians instead satisfy their own greed or will to power or feed feelings of self-importance. There can be no reasonable hope of change in the behavior of public officials unless voters reject faith as a method of selecting their beliefs regarding politicians and political processes. This amounts to a total rejection of faith, however, because there can be no legitimate reason why one would reject faith regarding one area and embrace it in others. Besides, habits formed for one purpose inevitably influence other matters, so it will all be the same even if one could separate different areas of thought into those in which faith is acceptable and those in which it is not. This becomes obvious when one considers, for example, the influence of one's religion on one's beliefs regarding biology. Biology is often regarded as a discipline in which faith is supposed to be irrelevant, but it is clear that one's faith influences one's beliefs about biology. We see in this country many people whose faith in their various forms of Christianity forces them to reject any form of evolutionary theory. Of course there are many types of Christians who see no conflict between their religions and various theories of evolution, but this only shows that where one's faith impinges on the various disciplines will be somewhat unpredictable and rather variable. It is not to be expected that these other Christians who have no difficulties with theories of evolution will not ultimately reject some other scientific theory—perhaps they might, for example, reject scientific theories regarding death. It is clear that beliefs in one area do affect other areas, and that, as Clifford states:

> No real belief, however trifling and fragmentary it may seem, is ever truly insignificant; it prepares us to receive more of its like, confirms those which resembled it before, and weakens others; and so gradually it lays a stealthy train in our inmost thoughts, which may some day explode into overt action, and leave its stamp upon our character for ever. [Vol. II, 181-182; *13 in this edition*]

It is clear from these remarks that it can be very beneficial for individuals to form their beliefs based upon evidence, for they may save their time and money by not wasting them on unworthy endeavors and products. It is also clear that it is beneficial to society as a whole, for, not only would there be an improvement in politics, there would also be fewer people ready to deceive, for there would be fewer gullible people ready to be cheated. Or, to put this in Clifford's words, "The credulous man is father to the liar and the cheat...." [Vol. II, 186; *17 in this edition*] Thus we see, by the rejection of faith, beneficial consequences both to ourselves and others. What could be more desirable than this?

Afterword

2008

Several readers have favored me with their responses to my essay and book, which have brought to my attention that some additional details are desirable for greater clarity. What follows are some summary comments which should alleviate some confusion that some of my readers have had.

1. Clifford *never* said that beliefs should be legislated; he said that what one believes is of ethical significance *because* belief is intimately tied to action. Being of ethical significance is entirely different from being something that should be legislated. Indeed, his requirement that individuals weigh evidence for themselves in order to determine what they should believe is directly contrary to the idea that particular beliefs should be required by law. Clifford's position, therefore, *requires freethinking*.

2. Pragmatism. The first thing to observe is that pragmatism is not mentioned in "The Will to Believe", which was first given as a lecture, and is the first essay in the book *The Will to Believe and other essays in popular philosophy*. James developed those ideas later (the book *Pragmatism* came out many years later). Furthermore, James mentions in "What Pragmatism Means" (in *Pragmatism*) that no one knew what pragmatism was at the time when "The Will to Believe" came out (he does not mention the essay by name; one has to compare the dates he mentions with the date of this essay). "The Will to Believe"

was presented as a lecture in 1896, and first published in 1897. In "What Pragmatism Means" (first delivered as a lecture in 1906 or 1907; and first printed in 1907), James stated:

> A glance at the history of the idea will show you still better what pragmatism means. The term is derived from the same Greek word πράγμα, meaning action, from which our words 'practice' and 'practical' come. It was first introduced into philosophy by Mr. Charles Peirce in 1878. ...
>
> This is the principle of Peirce, the principle of pragmatism. It lay entirely unnoticed by anyone for twenty years, until I, in an address before Professor Howison's philosophical union at the university of California, brought it forward again and made a special application of it to religion. By that date (1898) the times seemed ripe for its reception. [Pages 18-19 of the Dover Thrift Edition.]

According to James, pragmatism was first espoused by him in 1898, and had been previously "entirely unnoticed by anyone". That was the year *after* "The Will to Believe" was printed. So, according to James, his audience for "The Will to Believe" knew *absolutely nothing* about pragmatism. Consequently, James did not require an understanding of pragmatism to understand the essay "The Will to Believe" contained in this book. Therefore, I made no comment here about pragmatism and its virtues or vices, as it is irrelevant to the topic of this book.

3. Some of my readers have objected to my literary style and "tone". Be that as it may, it is irrelevant to the arguments presented, and I strongly advise the reader to

focus on the reasons presented rather than on literary style. It is the reasoning that matters, not the poetry of the words, or lack thereof. It is unfortunate that so many are swayed by pretty lies rather than by less pretty truths.

Shortly before this book first appeared in print, the World Trade Center was destroyed on September 11, 2001, with an aircraft flown into each of the two towers. The book was basically finished, but there were still some formatting issues to be settled. I considered adding this example to my discussion of James' position, which would have made the book timelier, but I decided at that time that it would, perhaps, be too unpleasant for some people to read, and it also seemed to me sufficiently obvious that the basic story of the official version of what happened is an example of something consistent with James' theory that it need not be mentioned. Since then, it has become clear that it is not obvious enough for some people, so I will presently examine that example here.

Let us consider, in the abstract, the possibility of people wondering, prior to September 11, 2001, whether or not God hates the U.S., and whether or not it would be God's will, and right and proper, and would earn an honored place in heaven, to destroy the World Trade Center by hijacking commercial airliners and crashing them into it.

First, it may be observed, that although it is probably not a *living hypothesis* for most of the people reading this, that does not mean that it could not be a *living hypothesis* for anyone. Just as one particular religion seems possible to some people, to others, it seems impossible and ridiculous.

It is certainly conceivable that some people would consider it possible. Presumably, it would also be a living hypothesis for such people not to believe that it was right and proper. So, for them, it would be a *living option*.

Second, they would either believe that it was right and proper to destroy the World Trade Center, or not, so it would also be a *forced option*.

Third, it would be a *momentous option*. Like James' generic example of the religious hypothesis, they would lose the honored place in heaven if they would forgo this opportunity. It is also rather important whether or not one kills a few thousand people.

And as a genuine option is one that is living, forced, and momentous, it would be a *genuine option*.

The next issue to consider is whether or not this genuine option is one "*that cannot by its nature be decided on intellectual grounds*." It is, of course, however distasteful to some, simply another religious view of the world, and consequently is as removed from the realm of evidence as religion typically is. It may, therefore, be considered to be as appropriate to believe, according to James' position, as any other religion.

The natural and obvious result of the belief that a particular action is right and proper is to do the action, so attempting the destruction of the World Trade Center is the result that should be expected from such a belief.

The obvious conclusion, therefore, is that attacking and destroying the World Trade Center would be a result of people perfectly following James' advice. This shows the practical outcome of James' advocacy of faith. This is the *cash value* of his theory. Those who encourage others to follow James' advice are encouraging actions like this.

Made in the USA
Monee, IL
28 December 2024

75546639R00066